The Doctor's Guide To Owning A Financially Healthy Practice:

What They Don't Teach You in Medical School

The Doctor's Guide To Owning A Financially Healthy Practice:

What They Don't Teach You in Medical School

Wayne A. Label, CPA, MBA, Ph.D.

Weldon E. Havins, MD, JD, MA (Mgmt)

Solana Dreams Publishing Company

Solana Beach, California

Order this book online at www.trafford.com
or email orders@trafford.com

Most Trafford titles are also available at major online book retailers.

Printed in the United States of America.

ISBN: 978-1-4269-3875-7

*Our mission is to efficiently provide the world's finest, most comprehensive book publishing
service, enabling every author to experience success. To find out how to publish your book,
your way, and have it available worldwide, visit us online at www.trafford.com*

Trafford rev. 7/14/2010

 www.trafford.com

North America & international
toll-free: 1 888 232 4444 (USA & Canada)
phone: 250 383 6864 • fax: 812 355 4082

Table of Contents

Acknowledgments

We would like to thank all the health care professionals who have reviewed this book and made helpful comments and to our families, Florencia, Kelly, Bradley, Laura and Anna.

We would also like to thank Valerie Higgins for making this book readable and grammatically correct and Jennifer Subbotin for her endless help in formatting, reviewing and preparing it for publication.

Introduction

Why do health care professionals need to know anything about accounting? How does it benefit businesses? Why can't health care professionals just "turn it all over" to the bookkeeper or accountant?

This book answers those questions for the medical professional.

Accounting provides information that helps people in business increase their chances of making good decisions that will benefit their companies. Accounting is the language of business, and like other languages, it has it own terms and rules. Understanding this language and learning to interpret it is your first step to becoming successful in your own business and in your personal financial life as well.

In your personal life you can use accounting information to make decisions about investing in the stock market, applying for a loan, and evaluating potential jobs. Banks use accounting information to make decisions about granting loans. Government agencies base their regulations on accounting information they receive from the nation's companies. Accounting information can even be useful to non-business entities with an interest in how businesses affect local, national, or foreign communities and community members. Businesses use accounting information for planning and budgeting and for making decisions about borrowing and investing. Overall, accounting aids businesses in the process of making better decisions.

The basics of accounting are the same regardless of the size or type of business. In The Doctor's Guide To Owning A Financially Healthy Practice: What They Don't Teach You In Medical School, you will learn the basics of accounting through the examination of an imaginary medical practice, Desert Medical Care Company. For more complex businesses, the economic transactions become more varied and complex as does the process of reporting them to various users. The foundation of it all, however, remains the same. This book will provide you with a solid accounting foundation you can apply to business questions you'll encounter in daily practice.

Especially if you have little or no experience with accounting and financial statements, this is the book for you.

Chapter 1

Introducing Accounting and Financial Statements

This chapter covers the following information:

✓ What Is Accounting?

✓ Who Uses Accounting Information?

✓ Financial Statements

✓ How Different Business Entities Present Accounting Information

What Is Accounting?

The purpose of accounting is to provide information that will help you make correct financial decisions. The accountant's job is to provide the information needed to run a business as efficiently as possible while maximizing profits and keeping costs low.

☞ Quick Tip:

Accounting plays a role in businesses of all sizes. Your kids' lemonade stand, a one-person business, and a multinational corporation all use the same basic accounting principles. Accounting is legislated; it affects your taxes; even the president plays a role in how accounting affects you. The list goes on and on.

Accounting is the language of business. It is the process of recording, classifying and summarizing economic events through certain documents or financial statements. Like any other language, accounting has its own terms and rules. To understand how to interpret and use the information accounting provides, you must first understand this language. Understanding the basic concepts of accounting is essential to success in business.

Different types of information furnished by accountants are shown in Figure 1.1 below.

Figure 1.1

Types of Information Provided by Accountants

- Information prepared exclusively by people within a firm (managers, employees, or owners) for their own use

- Financial information required by various government agencies such as the Internal Revenue Service (IRS), Securities and Exchange Commission (SEC), and the Federal Trade Commission (FTC)

- General information about companies provided to people outside the firm such as investors, creditors, and labor unions

Accounting and Bookkeeping

Bookkeeping procedures and a bookkeeper's records keep track of business transactions that are later used to generate financial statements. Most bookkeeping procedures have been systematized and in many cases can be handled by computer programs. This is particularly true in health care providers' businesses. Bookkeeping is a very important part of the accounting process, but it is just the beginning. There is currently no certification required to become a bookkeeper in the United States. Some proprietary bookkeeping software programs have their own certification programs. Some of these programs are online and available to any interested person. Anyone using a particular bookkeeping software would likely benefit from the investment in time and money to become certified.

Accounting is the process of preparing and analyzing financial statements based on the transactions recorded through the bookkeeping process. Accountants are usually professionals who have completed a bachelor's degree in accounting, and often have passed a professional examination, like the Certified Public Accountant Examination, the Certified Management Accountant Examination, or Certified Fraud Auditor Examination.

Accounting goes beyond bookkeeping and the recording of economic information to include the summarizing and reporting of this information in a way that is meant to drive decision making within a business.

Who Uses Accounting Information?

In the world of business, accounting plays an important role to aid in making critical decisions. The more complex the decision, the more detailed the information must be. Individuals and companies need different kinds of information to make their business decisions.

Let's start with you as an individual health care provider. Why would you be interested in accounting? In addition to the benefits to your business, accounting knowledge can help you with investing in the stock market, apply for a home loan, evaluating a potential job, balancing a check book, and starting a personal savings plan, among other things.

Managers within a business also use accounting information daily to make decisions although most of these managers are not accountants. Some of the decisions they might make for which they will use accounting information are illustrated in figure 1.2.

Figure 1.2

Areas in Which Managers Use Accounting Information

- Marketing (Which line of services should the company emphasize?)

- Production (Should the company provide services in one location or open several locations?)

- Research and Development (How much money should be set aside for new skills development?)

- Sales (Should the company expand the advertising budget and take money away from some other part of the marketing budget?)

Without the proper accounting information these types of decisions would be very difficult, if not impossible, to make. Bankers continually use accounting information. They are in the business of taking care of your money and making money with your money, so they absolutely must make good decisions. Accounting is fundamental to their decision-making process. Figure 1.3 looks at some of the decisions bankers make using accounting information.

Figure 1.3

Areas in Which Bankers Use Accounting Information

- Granting loans to individuals and companies

- Investing clients' money

- Setting interest rates

- Meeting federal regulations for protecting your money

Government agencies such as the Internal Revenue Service (IRS), the Securities and Exchange Commission (SEC), the Federal Trade Commission (FTC), the Bureau of Alcohol, Tobacco and Firearms (ATF) base their regulation enforcement and compliance on the accounting information they receive.

Accountability in Accounting

A business's financial statements can also be of great interest to other members of the local or sometimes even the national community. Labor groups might be interested in what impact management's financial decisions have on their unions and other employees. Local communities have an interest in how a business's financial decisions (for example, layoffs or facility closings) will impact their citizens.

As the economy becomes more complex, so do the transactions within a business and the process of reporting them to various users and of making them understandable become more complex as well. A solid knowledge of accounting is helpful to individuals, managers, and business owners who are making their decisions based on the information accounting documents provide.

Financial Statements

Accountants supply information to people both inside and outside the firm by issuing formal reports that are called financial statements.

The financial statements are usually issued at least once a year. In many cases they are issued quarterly or more often where necessary. A set of rules, called Generally Accepted Accounting Principles, govern the preparation of the financial statements. Generally Accepted Accounting Principles (GAAP) has been defined as a set of objectives, conventions, and principles to govern the preparation and presentation of financial statements. These rules can be found in volumes of documents issued by the American Institute of Certified Public

Accountants (AICPA), the Financial Accounting Standards Board (FASB), the Internal Revenue Service (IRS), the Securities and Exchange Commission (SEC), and other regulatory bodies. In Chapter 2 we look at some of the over-riding principles of Accounting as they apply to all businesses and individuals.

The Basic Financial Statements

The basic financial statements include the Balance Sheet, the Income Statement, the Statement of Retained Earnings, and The Statement of Cash Flows. We will look at these in depth in the following Chapters and see how they all interact with each other. As we discuss these financial statements, you will see they are not as scary as you might have thought they would be. Many of the concepts will already be familiar to you.

In the Appendix, you can see examples of these financial statements from a typical medical practice.

The Balance Sheet is the statement that presents the assets of the company (those items owned by the company) and the liabilities (those items owed to others by the company).

The Income Statement shows all of the revenues of the company less the expenses, to arrive at the "bottom line", the net income.

The Statement of Cash Flows shows how much cash we started the period with, what additions and subtractions were made during the period, and how much cash we have left over at the end of the period. This is often the most difficult of the accounting statements for the health care provider to understand. We'll explain why and simplify reading cash flow statements.

The Statement of Retained Earnings shows how the balance in Retained Earnings has changed during the period of time (year, quarter, month) for which the financial statements are being prepared.

Normally there are only two types of events that will cause the beginning balance to change: 1) the company makes a profit, which causes an increase in Retained Earnings (or the company suffers a loss, which would cause a decrease) and 2) the owners of the company withdraw money which causes the beginning balance to decrease (or invest more money which will cause it to increase).

↪Alert

Seeing the Bigger Picture: None of these financial statements alone can tell the whole story about a company. We need to know how to read, understand, and analyze these statements as a package in order to make any kind of decisions about the company. In addition to the financial statements, you must understand the industry in which you are operating and the general economy.

Financial statements vary in form depending upon the type of business in which they are used. In general there are three forms of business operating in the United States – proprietorships, partnerships, and corporations. These are the basic business forms for health care providers' businesses.

How Different Business Entities Present Accounting Information

Proprietorships are businesses with a single owner like you or me. These types of businesses tend to be small service business started by what can be called "entrepreneurs." The accounting for these proprietorships includes only the records of the business - not the personal financial records of the proprietor of the business.

↳Alert

Partnerships are very similar to proprietorships, except that instead of one owner there are two or more owners. In general most of these businesses are small to medium-sized. However, there are some exceptions, such as large groups or even national chains that may have thousands of partners. As with the proprietorships, accounting treats these organizations' records as separate and distinct from those of the individual partners.

Finally, there are corporations. These are businesses that are owned by one or more stockholders. Any particular owner may or may not have a managerial interest in the company. Many of these stockholders are simply owners who have money invested in the company by way of stocks which they have purchased.

In a corporation, a person becomes an owner by buying shares in the company and thus becomes a stockholder. The stockholders may or may not have a vote in the company's long-term planning depending on the type of stock they have purchased. However, simply by being stockholders (owners), they do not have decision making authority in the day-to-day operations. These investors (or stockholders) are not much different than the bankers that loan money to a proprietorship or a partnership. These bankers have a financial interest in the business, but no daily managerial decision making power. As is the case with the stockholders who have invested money into the corporation, in general they have a non-managerial interest in the business. As with the other two types of business organizations discussed here, the accounting records of the corporation are maintained separately from those of the individual stockholders, or owners.

The accounting records of a proprietorship are less complex than those of a corporation in that there is a simple capital structure with only one owner. In the case of a corporation, there are stockholders, which buy a piece of the ownership of a company by buying stock. As we will discuss later, because of this stock ownership, the financial statements become more complex. Some of the basic differences between these three types of businesses are shown below in Figure 1.4.

Figure 1.4

Differences in the Three Types of Businesses

Business Type	Proprietorship	Partnership	Corporation
Number of Owners	One	Two or more	One or more
Accounting Records	Maintained separately from owner's records	Maintained separately from owners' records	Maintained separately from owner's records
Owner Has Managerial Responsibilities	Yes	Usually	Usually not

In this Chapter you have learned what accounting is, why you and other people in health care provider business need to understand accounting, what businesses use accounting for, and what the basic financial statements used in these businesses are. In Chapter 2 you will learn about the principles used by accountants in the United States as well a comparison of those used by accountants in most other countries in the world (as prescribed by the International Accounting Standards Board located in London, England).

Glossary

Accounting: The process of recording, classifying and summarizing economic events through the preparation of financial statements such as the balance sheet, the income statement and the statement of cash flows.

American Institute of Certified Public Accountants (AICPA): The professional organization of CPAs in the United States. The AICPA is charged with preparation of the CPA Examination, the establishment and enforcement of the code of professional ethics, and working with the Financial Accounting Standards Board in the proclamation of accounting standards.

Corporations: Corporations are businesses that are given the right to exist by an individual state in the United States. With this right to exist, the corporation is then allowed to issue stock. Those buying this stock become owners of the corporation. Corporations can be set up as for profit or not for profit, and make that decision when applying for their charter with the state.

Financial Accounting Standards Board (FASB): The FASB sets the accounting standards to be followed for the preparation of financial statements. All rulings from the FASB are considered to be GAAP.

Financial Statements: Reports prepared by companies on the financial status of their business; examples are balance sheets, income statements, statement of cash flow, and statement of retained earnings.

Generally Accepted Accounting Principles (GAAP): The rules that govern the preparation of financial statements. These rules are developed by the American Institute of Certified Public Accountants, the Financial Accounting Standards Board, the Security and Exchange Commission, and other government agencies.

Internal Revenue Service (IRS): The government agency charged with the collection of federal taxes in the United States. There are different accounting rules for the preparation of taxes in the United States than for the presentation of financial statements. (GAAP)

Partnerships: A business entity with one or more owners. The accounting for partnerships is similar to that of proprietorships.

Proprietorships, sole proprietorships: Businesses with one single owner. Even though there is only one owner, the records of the owner's personal financial affairs are kept separate from those of the accounting records of the business. Separate tax returns are prepared for the business and for the individual.

Statement of Retained Earnings: A financial statement that shows how the balance in Retained Earnings has changed during the period of time (year, quarter, month) for which the financial statements are being prepared.

Chapter 2

Generally Accepted Accounting Principles

This chapter covers the following information:

✓ Who Are the SEC, AICPA, FASB AND IASB?

✓ Generally Accepted Accounting Principles (GAAP)

✓ International Accounting Standards (IAS)

It is important that you understand the concepts of Generally Accepted Accounting Principles (GAAP) which form the basis of accounting and are part of the language of accounting and business. Third parties, who invest or provide loans to any company, must know that they can rely on the financial information provided.

This chapter will introduce the agencies responsible for standardizing the accounting principles that are used in the United States and will describe those principles in full detail. Once you understand these guiding principles, you will have a solid foundation on which to build a complete set of accounting skills. It is useful and necessary that whether an international company is reporting to its stockholders, or a proprietor is presenting information to a bank for a loan. These reports follow a consistent set of rules that everyone understands and to which everyone agrees.

Who Are the SEC, AICPA, and The FASB? (or What Is This Alphabet Soup?)

Congress created the Securities and Exchange Commission (SEC) in 1934. At that time, the Commission was given the legal power to prescribe the accounting principles and practices that must be followed by the companies that come within its jurisdiction. Generally speaking, companies come under SEC regulations when a) they sell securities to the public, b) list their securities on any one of the securities exchanges (New York Stock Exchange or American Exchange for example) or c) when they become greater than a specified size as measured by the firm's assets and number of shareholders. Thus, since 1934, the SEC has had the power to determine the official rules of accounting practice that must be followed by almost all companies of any significant size.

Instead, for the most part, the SEC assigned the responsibility of identifying or specifying GAAP to the American Institute of Certified Public Accountants (AICPA). That role has now been transferred to the Financial Accounting Standards Board (FASB). All rulings from the FASB are considered to be GAAP.

A firm must adopt the accounting practices recommended by the FASB or the SEC unless they can identify an alternative practice that has "substantial authoritative support." Even when a company can find "substantial authoritative support" for a practice it uses which differs from the one recommended, the company must include in the financial statement footnotes (or in the auditor's report) a statement indicating that the practices used are not the ones recommended by GAAP. Where practicable, the company must explain how its financial statements would have been different if the company had used Generally Accepted Accounting Principles.

Generally Accepted Accounting Principles (GAAP)

To better understand Generally Accepted Accounting Principles, note that there are three basic assumptions made about each business. First, it is assumed that the business is separate from its owners or other businesses. Revenue and expenses should be kept separate from personal expenses.

Second, it is assumed that the business will be in operation indefinitely. This validates the methods of putting assets on the Balance Sheet, depreciation and amortization. Only when liquidation of a business is certain, does this assumption no longer apply.

Third, it is assumed a business' accounting records include only quantifiable transactions. Certain economic events that affect a company, such as hiring a new employee or introducing a new product or service, cannot be quantified in monetary units and, therefore, do not appear in a company's accounting records.

↪ Alert

Accounting records must always be recorded using a stable currency. In the U.S. this is the dollar, in Europe it is the Euro, etc.

Financial statements must present relevant, reliable, understandable, sufficient, and practicably obtainable information in order to be useful.

Category (A) (Most Authoritative)	FASB Standards and Interpretations	Accounting Principles Board (APB) Opinions	AICPA Accounting Research Bulletins (ARBs)
Category (B)	FASB Technical Bulletins	AICPA Industry Audit and Accounting	AICPA Statements of Position

		Guides	(SOPs)
Category (C)	FASB	Emerging Issues Task Force (EITF)	AICPA AcSEC Practice Bulletins
Category (D) (Least Authoritative)	AICPA Accounting Interpretations	FASB Implementation Guides (Q & A)	Widely recognized and prevalent industry practices

Table: www.aicpa.org

Relevant Information

Relevant information is that information which helps financial statement users estimate the value of a firm and/or evaluate how well the firm is being managed. The financial statements must be stated in terms of a monetary unit, since money is our standard means of determining the value of a company.

In the United States, accountants use the stable monetary unit concept which means that even though the value of the dollar changes over time (due to inflation), the values that appear on the financial statements normally are presented at historical cost. Historical cost presents the information on the financial statements at amounts the individual or company paid for them or agreed to pay back for them at the time of purchase. This method of accounting ignores the effect of inflation. In many other countries throughout the world, the accounting profession does account for inflation.

↪ Alert

Changes in the Works: In August 2008, the Security and Exchange Commission announced that within the next decade the US will abandon GAAP, used by accountants for almost 75 years, and join the more than 100 countries worldwide in using IFRS (discussed in detail on page 33). A timetable was set for all US companies to drop GAAP by 2016, with some larger companies in the US possibly switching in 2009. Yet, things can still change, and many questions are still unanswered. When or whether smaller businesses such as those typically owned by health care practitioners will transfer to IFRS accounting has yet to be determined.

Not all information about a firm is relevant for estimating its value or evaluating its management. For example, you don't need the information of how many individuals over forty years of age work for the company, or what color the equipment is painted in order to make financial decisions about a company. Even some financial information is not relevant, like how much money the owner of a corporation has in his or her personal bank account because, as we reviewed in Chapter 1, the business's accounting records are kept separate from its owner's, and the owner's financial information is irrelevant to the business.

Reliable Information

Reliable information is key in accounting. Sufficient and objective evidence should be available to indicate that the information presented is valid. In addition, the information must not be biased in favor of one statement user or one group of users to the detriment of other statement users. The need for reliable information has caused the federal government to pass laws requiring public companies to have their records and financial statements examined (audited) by independent auditors who will make sure that what companies report is accurate. This will be the topic of Chapter 11.

Verifiable Information

The need for verifiable information does not preclude the use of estimates and approximation. If you were to eliminate from accounting all estimates, the resulting statements would not be useful primarily because the statements would not provide sufficient information. The approximations that are used, however, cannot be "wild guesses." They must be based on sufficient evidence to make the resulting statements a reliable basis for evaluating the firm and its management.

One example of a place in the financial statements where we estimate the value is with depreciation. Once we purchase a long-term asset (anything that the company owns that will last longer than one year, for example a building), we then need to spread the cost of this building over the life of the asset. This is called depreciation. In order to do this we must estimate the life of that particular asset. We can't know exactly how long that will be, but since we do have experience with these types of assets, we can estimate the asset's life. We assume that the building will be useable for say 20 years and depreciate (or spread) the cost of the building (the asset) over 20 years (the estimated life).

For example, if we buy this building for $100,000, and assume that it is going to last 20 years, the annual depreciation would be $5,000 per year ($100,000/ 20). This $5,000 becomes one of the expenses for the company and is shown on the income (or profit and loss) statement along with the other expenses. We will look at this topic in depth in Chapter 4.

Understandable Information

To be understandable, the financial information must be comparable. Any item on the Balance Sheet that an accountant labels as an asset or liability, users of the financial statements should also call assets and liabilities. Statement users must compare financial statements of various entities with one another, and they must compare statements of an individual entity with prior years' statements of that same entity in order to make valid decisions. Thus, the accounting practices that an entity uses for a particular transaction should be the same as other entities use for the identical transaction. This practice should also be the same practice the entity used in previous periods. This concept is called Consistency. Together, information that is comparable and consistent becomes understandable to the users of the financial information.

Quantifiable Information

"If you can't measure it, you can't manage it" is a frequent homily to emphasize the importance of quantifiable information. Most information that accountants and users of financial information use is represented by numbers. The information that is presented in the financial statements is presented in a numerical form; however, where that is impossible, the information (if it is relevant, reliable, understandable, and practicably obtainable) will be presented in narrative form, usually in a footnote to the statements. Accountants include narrative information along with the quantifiable information. Because of the need for adequate or full disclosure; statement users must have sufficient information about an entity.

An example of non-quantifiable information that might be included in the footnotes to the financial statements would be an outstanding lawsuit against the company, such as a patent infringement. This is an example of a contingent liability.

Obtainable Information

Furthermore, to be useful, information must be reasonably easy to obtain. This fits into the concept of cost v. benefit. The information must be worth more than what it will cost to obtain it and must be secured on a timely basis. Financial statements must be prepared at least once a year (in many cases, quarterly or monthly) and attempting to incorporate unobtainable information could seriously delay these schedules.

An example of obtainable information is the amount of revenue from business during the year. An example of information that might not be considered obtainable would be the nitty-gritty details of the pension plan systems used in each of the subsidiaries of a multi-national corporation. A more reasonable and easily obtainable piece of data might be the total amount of money that is being spent on the company's pensions.

The Entity Concept

Financial statements must present information representing each separate entity. (This idea is called the Entity Concept). In other words, the transactions of each business or person are kept separate from those of other organizations or individuals. Therefore, the transactions of the subsidiaries of a corporation must all be kept separate from each other. Even though at the end of the year, the records of all of the subsidiaries might be consolidated into one set of financial statements, the records and transactions of each subsidiary are kept separate during the year.

The Going Concern

It is normally assumed that a company will continue in business into the future. This concept is called the Going Concern Principle. There are several estimates that we make in order to complete the financial statement presentations (for example depreciation of an asset over its life), and if we did not assume that the company was going to remain in business in the indefinite future, we could not use this sort of information.

The alternative to the Going Concern Principle is to assume that the Management plans to liquidate the business. When this is known for sure about a business, a different set of accounting principles and rules are used. In general when a company liquidates, the assets of the company will be listed at what they can be sold at rapidly. This amount will usually be below their values stated on the balance sheet, since they will be sold at "fire sale" prices.

Realizable Value

Assets normally are not shown on the Balance Sheet at more than either their historical cost or an amount for which they can be sold below historical cost. For example, if a company has inventory that is listed at a historical cost of $100,000, but due to the economy, the competition, or new technology, is today only worth $8,000, this asset should be written down and shown on the Balance Sheet at $8,000. The section on conservatism (page tk) sheds more light on this topic. An example of an exception to this rule is with marketable securities (stocks). These assets are shown on the Balance Sheet at their current market price.

➥Alert

Accounting Outside the U.S.: In the United States, for the purpose of preparing financial statements, accountants are not allowed to write up assets to value higher than the historical cost. This is not true in all countries of the world, where accountants may argue that if you can write down an asset to reflect "reality," why not do the same when an asset increases in value? Thus, in many countries outside of the United States, the accountants are allowed to write up assets when they increase in value to reflect "market value", as well as write them down when the market value is lower than historical cost. This is an important point to keep in mind when reviewing financial statements prepared in companies domiciled outside of the United States.

Materiality

Financial statements' data must be as simple and concise as possible. An item is considered material when its inclusion or exclusion in the financial statements would change the decision of a statement user. A rule of thumb in accounting might be that any item worth 10 percent of the business's net income is considered material and should be reported in financial statements; there is no firm dollar amount to be followed here. The important factor to remember is whether the amount in question will change the user's decision. This concept is called the Materiality Principle.

Items that are not material should not be included on the statements separately. If these items were included in the financial statements they would obscure the important items of interest to the reader. Thus, in some cases, many immaterial items should be grouped together and called "miscellaneous" or the items could be added to other items, so that the total becomes material. That is, the items can be lumped in together with other items which are material and the entire bundle can be considered material.

Conservatism

Another traditional practice that accountants use to guide them in preparing financial statements is called Conservatism. Whenever two or more accounting practices appear to be equally suitable to record the transaction under consideration, the accountant should choose the one that results in the lower or lowest asset figure on the Balance Sheet and the higher or highest expense on the Income Statement so as not be overly optimistic about financial events. This principle of accounting is highly controversial since while being conservative, we may be violating other generally accepted accounting principles like consistency. In addition it is often asked, "Why is the lower value better, if the higher value better represents the true value of the asset?"

An example of the Conservatism Principle in action might be in the presentation of inventory on the balance sheet. There are several different generally accepted accounting methods that are allowed to assign a value to inventory. The accountant should choose the one that presents inventory at the lowest value so as not to overstate this particular asset.

The conservatism idea is misused, however, when the accountant chooses a practice that is not as suitable to the situation as an alternative practice merely to report lower assets and higher expenses.

Quiz

The owners of a business decides to write up the value of their land, which 10 years ago cost $10,000 to purchase and today sits in a prime location of the city and has been appraised at $40,000. Should they value her land on the balance sheet at $10,000 or $40,000?

Answers are provided at the end of this chapter.

GAAP and Small Business

Small business owners have been asking for alternatives to GAAP for a long time. The feeling is that the GAAP used for public companies are irrelevant to small businesses and are very difficult and expensive to implement. The solution of some people is a separate set of standards for private companies—one that takes their needs specifically into account.

The FASB listened and appointed a committee in September 2006 to investigate the differences in reporting and accounting between private and public companies. It was determined that the final goal was to give small businesses a greater voice in standard setting and not to establish two sets of standards.

The Committee decided that it was not in the best interest of the public to have two classes of GAAP. They determined that two sets of standards would not only be confusing to the public, but also create the possibility of one set being considered more authoritative to the other.

International Financial Reporting Standards (IFRS)

International Financial Reporting Standards are issued by the International Accounting Standards Board (IASB), a committee of fourteen members from different countries headquartered in London. The Board has the goal of creating global accounting standards that are transparent, enforceable, understandable, and of high quality. More than 100 countries currently use or coordinate with IFRS.

This Board and the standards that they issue are very important for the future of accounting. As globalization continues to connect businesses across the world, it is increasingly important for investors to be able to compare companies under similar standards. It is also much more cost efficient for a company doing business in several different countries to issue one set of financial statements that is understood in all of those countries, rather than having to use the accounting standards of each country.

A great benefit of the IFRS is that it puts all companies in all countries on a level playing field since they all have to present their financial information in a consistent, reliable manner. This certainly makes the comparison of their financial results more comparable.

Differences between US GAAP and IFRS

The biggest difference between US GAAP and the International Accounting Standards is that the US standards are based on rules and the International Standards are based upon principles. So what does this mean? It means that the US standards have created a complex system of rules attempting to cover every situation that does or might occur, often masking economic reality. The US rules fill a nine-inch, three-volume set of guidelines, while the International Standards are inside a 2-inch book.

The principles-based system of accounting encourages company boards and accountants to do the right thing in allowing them to report what is correct for the user, rather than reporting based upon a set of rules. US GAAP rules allowed trillions of dollars in securitized financial assets and liabilities to stay off the books of U.S. financial firms, while the international standards, more focused on the true underlying economics, kept these items on the books of firms based outside the U.S.

The upcoming change to IFRS is going to be enormous for US companies in dollars and methodology. While there will be some ambiguity in the reporting, the accountant will need to explain why certain reporting standards have been used for more accuracy.

Based upon the European experience, it is believed that this switchover could be made in three years. In 2005, all 7,000 of the European Union's listed corporations switched from their home-country GAAP to IFRS and separate country GAAPs no longer exist.

Answer:

> In the United States a company cannot write the value of their assets above the historical cost of that asset. The argument is that if they do write the value, it leaves too much room for manipulating the financial statements which could mislead the users of the financial statements.

The practice of writing up assets, even though accepted in other countries, would violate such generally accepted accounting principles as; 1) conservatism, 2) reliability and 3) verifiability.

Glossary

American Institute of Certified Public Accountants (AICPA): The professional organization of the Accounting profession. This group has the responsibility to set the ethics regulations for the profession as well as writing and grading the certification public accountants' examination (CPA Examination).

Conservatism Principle: Whenever two or more accounting practices appear to be equally suitable to the transaction under consideration, the accountant should always choose the one that result in the lower or lowest asset figure on the Balance Sheet and the higher or highest expense on the Income Statement.

Consistency: Practices and methods used for presentation on the financial statements should be the same year to year and process to process. If for any reason the company and their accountants decide to change the method of presentation for any item on the financial statements, they must present a footnote to the financial statements explaining why the methods were changed.

Entity Concept: The principle that requires separation of the transactions of each business or person from those of other organizations or individuals. So for example, when a company is owned by one person, the personal finances of the individual who owns the company are not included on the company's financial statements. The opposite is also true, that the financial information of the company is not included in the financial statements of the individual owner.

Financial Accounting Standards Board (FASB): The FASB sets the accounting standards to be followed for the preparation of financial statements. All rulings from the FASB are considered to be GAAP.

Generally Accepted Accounting Principles (GAAP): A standardized set of accounting rules used in the United States and prescribed by various organizations, like the FASB and the SEC. These rules guide the uniform preparation of financial statements.

Going Concern Principle: This principle assumes that a company will continue in business into the future. Without this assumption most of the accounting information could not be presented in the financial statements since we are always making assumptions, like what is the life of a long-term asset. The only way to make this assumption is to further assume that the business will be in existence into the indefinite future.

Historical Cost Principle: According to this rule, most assets and liabilities should be represented on the balance sheet at the amount that was paid to acquire the asset, or for the liabilities, at the amount that was contracted to be paid in the future. No account is taken for either inflation or changing value of assets over time.

Materiality Principle: This principle states that an item should only be included on the Balance Sheet if it would change any decisions of a statement user. If, for example, a multi-million dollar corporation were to donate $100 to a charity, this information would not change any decision that management or an owner would make. However, since corporate money was spent, this distribution of the $100 must be combined with other small expenditures and reported as a "miscellaneous expense."

International Accounting Standards Board (IASB): This board responsible for setting the International Accounting Standards used by more than 100 countries throughout the world. It is made up of 14 members from around the world and is based in London.

International Financial Reporting Standards (IFRS): The standards issued by IASB, meant to level the playing field for better comparisons of financial data as companies become more global in their scope.

Monetary Unit: Since a business' accounting records can only include quantifiable transactions, these transactions need to be reported in a stable currency, such as US Dollars, Euros, Yen, etc.

Obtainable Information: This principle states that information reported in financial statements must be accessible in a timely manner without an unreasonable expenditure of resources – for example, time, effort, and money – to be included in the financial statements.

Quantifiable Information: Information is easier to understand and use if it is quantified. However, when the information can-not be quantified but is still relevant to the users of the financial statements, it must be shown in the financial statements in narrative form in the footnotes.

Realizable Value Principle: This indicates that assets should normally not be shown on the Balance Sheet at a value greater than they can bring to the company if sold. If the original historical cost for example is $5,000.00, and the maximum that the company can sell that asset for today is $4,000.00, this asset should be shown on the balance sheet at the lower amount because of this principle.

Relevant information: Information reported on financial statements must be relevant in that it helps statement users to estimate the value of a firm and/or evaluate the firm's management. Not all information about a company is relevant to this decision making process. For example, the number of women versus men currently employed at the company would not be considered relevant, even though it might be important data in other contexts. Thus, this type of information is not included in the financial statements.

Securities and Exchange Commission (SEC): The body created by Congress in 1934. Part of their duties are to prescribe the accounting principles and practices that must be followed by the companies that come within its jurisdiction.

Recognition Principle: This is the process of recording revenue into the financial statements. Under GAAP, revenue is recorded at the point of the transfer of the merchandise or service, and not at the point of receiving the cash. That means that, for example, once a service is provided for which a charge has been incurred, that service should be shown on the financial statements regardless of whether money has actually changed hands. Similarly, expenses are recognized when incurred, not when the money is exchanged for that particular expense. Because of the particular nature of health care provider practices, and in an effort to more accurately portray the status of the health care entity, a modified recognition system, known as modified cash basis accounting is often used. Under this system, revenue is recognized when cash is received, while liabilities are recognized when they are incurred (not when payment for the liability is made).

Reliable Information: There should be sufficient and objective evidence available to indicate that the information presented is valid.

Separate Entities: See Entity Concept

Stable-Monetary-Unit Concept: Even though the value of the dollar changes over time (due to inflation), the values that appear on the financial statements in the United States are normally presented at historical cost and do not take inflation into account.

Understandable Information: Financial information must be comparable and consistent. If one accountant calls a particular item an asset, the accountant must follow the set of rules known as generally accepted accounting principles to arrive at the definition of that asset. Thus, when any user of the financial statements reads these statements, they understand the meaning and classification of the asset.

Verifiable Information: Information on the financial statements must be based on sufficient evidence which can be substantiated and which provides a reliable basis for evaluating the firm and its management.

Chapter 3

The Balance Sheet: Why Does it Have to Balance?

This chapter covers the following information:

✓ Understanding the Balance Sheet

✓ The Accounting Equation

✓ The Components of the Balance Sheet

✓ The Transactions Behind the Balance Sheet

Understanding the Balance Sheet

Imagine that you make a list of everything that is important to you. Along with this list you attach values to all of these items. Then you make a list of everything that you owe to others, and again you attach values to these items. Then you subtract the total value of the second list from the total value of the first. Voila! You have just created the basic components of a Balance Sheet.

In modified cash basis accounting, such as most health providers' business use, a bill is submitted for services rendered. There is an expectation of payment, but that payment to be received may be substantially less than the billing due to allowable discounts or insurance. Therefore, in the modified cash basis accounting method, income is not recognized until payment is received. This is a form of not counting your chickens until the eggs have hatched.

In a business, the first list of items is called Assets. Assets are valuable resources owned by the business and can be either short- or long-term in nature.

Your second list of items is called Liabilities. Liabilities are what you owe to others for resources that were furnished to the business. The parties to whom the company owes money are normally called creditors. The creditors are said to "have a claim against the assets." Figure 3.1 illustrates the origin of some liabilities a company or individual might incur.

Figure 3.1

Where Do Liabilities Come From?

Where Liabilities Originate	What they are called
Services from employees, not yet paid	Wages payable
Loans from Banks	Notes Payable
IOUs	Notes Payable
Interest owed on loans from banks	Interest Payable

Your third list can be labeled Owner's Equity. Owner's Equity reflects the amount the owner has invested in the firm. There are two sources of Owner's Equity:

• The amount of money provided directly by the owner or other investors, called Owner's Investment and

• The amount retained from profits, called Retained Earnings.

↪Alert

Profit takes many forms: Profits are not always cash; profit can be made up of promises to pay money as well. For example, when there is a sale for a receivable, there will be standard accrual accounting revenue, but no cash coming into the company now. The money will come in during a later time period but can be considered profit for the company now. In modified cash basis accounting, profit would not be realized until cash was received for the sale. Thus, in modified cash basis accounting, the accounting method most used in medical practices, assets applying to increase profits are not recognized in the Balance Sheet until those assets (cash) are actually received by the medical practice. Money earned but not yet received, such as occurs when insurance is billed but the payment from the insurance company has not been received, is not recognized as an asset of the medical practice.

Let's look at an example. The Desert Medical Care Company is a small business that provides medical services. Dr. Sarah Lawrence started the company in January 2011. Dr. Sarah (as all of her friends call her) has been a pediatrician for many years and has always wanted to start her own clinic providing various medical services to the local community. Dr. Sarah invested some money she had saved and some that she had inherited into her new clinic.

Take a look at the Company's balance sheet in Figure 3.2. This is a sole proprietorship, because Dr. Sarah is the sole owner of the company. The balance sheet would look a little different for a partnership or a corporation. These differences are discussed in Chapter 7.

Figure 3.2

DESERT MEDICAL CARE COMPANY

Balance Sheet

December 31, 2011

ASSETS

Cash...$9,050
Money Market Account.............................50,000
Security Deposit.....................................10,000
Supplies...60,950
Computers..45,000
Electronic Medical Records Software................45,000
Furniture and Equipment...........................100,000
Total Assets... $320,000

LIABILITIES AND OWNERS EQUITY

Liabilities: Taxes $6,000
           Salaries 5,000
           Bank 200,000
           Retirement 10,000
Total Liabilities.. $221,000

Owner's Equity   Owner's Investment...................120,000

           Retained Earnings.....................(21,000)
           Total Owner's Equity.................$99,000
Total Liabilities & Owner's Equity........................... $320,000

By looking at the medical company's Balance Sheet, you can see that there are several assets belonging to the company that together are valued at $320,000. You can also see that the company has several liabilities, valued at $221,000. Finally, when you subtract the liabilities from the assets, you can see that the company has equity (also referred to as net worth) of $99,000. This represents a combination of the amount of money that the owner has invested into her business ($120,000), and the net loss that was incurred in the first year of operations ($21,000).

What Does the Date on the Balance Sheet Mean?

There is a great deal of disagreement as to how accountants arrive at the values that are shown above on the balance sheet. Of most concern are the values attached to the assets, and consequently to the Owner's Equity or net worth of the business. The balance sheet represents a "snapshot" of the financial position of the business on that specific date. In the case of Desert Medical Care Company this point in time is December 31, 2011.

➥Alert

The Balance Sheet Is a Snapshot: The numbers that are represented in a balance sheet ONLY represent the financial position of the business at the exact point in time for which the balance sheet was prepared and no other. In Figure 3.2, this means December 31, 2011 only, not December 30 or January 1. On any other date there might be more or fewer assets and liabilities, and thus the balance sheet would look different. Remember also that this is modified cash accounting basis, not traditional accrual accounting. The numbers would look different in accrual accounting. The type of accounting is less important than using the same accounting month to month and year to year, so that you can compare "apples to apples, and oranges to oranges."

What Is Historical Cost?

As you saw above, all of the items on the Balance Sheet have values attached to them, but where did these numbers come from? In the United States, accountants and other users of financial statements have agreed that financial statements (including balance sheets) must be based on historical cost.

This means that the values on the Balance Sheet for Desert Medical Care Company do not represent what the assets or the liabilities would be worth today if they were to be sold. Instead the values represent what was paid for the assets and what the business agreed to pay to the banks on the date of the obligation.

Does this confuse the reader of the financial statements? No, because everyone has agreed to follow this convention. Everyone preparing and using these financial statements understands the language that is being spoken.

The Accounting Equation

Often the relationships between assets (A), liabilities (L) and owner's equity (OE) are shown in terms of a formula,

$$A = L + OE$$
$$\textbf{Assets = Liabilities + Owner's Equity}$$

The total assets of the company equal the sum of the liabilities and the owner's equity.

The formula depicts the relationships of the various elements of the Balance Sheet. Balance Sheets are often set up with the assets on one side (the left side) and the liabilities and equity on the other (the right side).

The same formula can be stated this way:

$$A - L = OE$$
$$\textbf{Assets} - \textbf{Liabilities} = \textbf{Owner's Equity}$$

If you subtract the liabilities from the assets, you are left with the owner's equity of the business.

The Components of the Balance Sheet

Assets

As was discussed above, assets are items of value and are owned by the entity for which you are accounting. Let's make this idea more specific. For an asset to be listed on a Balance Sheet of a company, the item must pass three tests.

Figure 3.3

How Do We Know When An Asset Goes on the Balance Sheet?

The following items give us some hints:

• The Company must control the item.
(This usually means ownership.)
• The item must have some value to the company.

• The item must have value that can be measured.

Let's look at some examples. Because of the first test, a traditional Balance Sheet does not list the employees of a company, even though we may refer to them as "assets" in a non-accounting sense, although the company does control, to a certain extent, but does not own these individuals. But what about the value of basketball players or other professional athletes? Doesn't the team own them? The answer is no. What the team owns is not the players themselves, but the players' contracts. Therefore, in this situation, the basketball team ownership would list the contracts of the players as an asset.

With the second test, almost anything that is used in the business to earn income and to generate cash does have some value. Certain items that do meet the first requirement might be eliminated from being listed as assets by this test. Examples might include an old truck that does not work or inventory that cannot be sold any longer because it is now outdated, such as an old version of computer software.

An example of the third test would be when the company purchases a used machine. The company purchased it for a fixed amount of money and the company has a record of this transaction, which clearly indicates the value of the machine. (Note: Neither the company nor the balance sheet deals with an over- or under-paid amount for the machine. The balance sheet reflects only historical cost, which is what is recorded as the amount paid for the machine, whether the company paid too much or got a bargain!)

Let's assume that a company has built up a thriving business, and some of the reasons for this growth are the reputation of the physician and the location of the company (medical practice). Neither the reputation of the physician nor the location of the company has been paid for, nor do we have any way of measuring a value to put onto these items. Therefore, they fail the third test, and cannot be listed as assets of the business.

Another example of an asset that would fail the test is any asset that was given to the company. In this situation, there is no historical cost to the company and thus the asset would not be reflected on the balance sheet, since it does not meet this third test. Now, you might say that we can determine a monetary value for this asset. And you are right! In many countries, this asset would then be reflected on the balance sheet at that value. However, under generally accepted accounting principles in the United States, since there was no historical cost to this asset, it would not be listed as one of the company's assets.

Quiz

Below is a list of items that might be considered assets by a company. Indicate whether they should be listed on the balance sheet as an asset and why or why not.

1. A car that belongs to the owner of the company

2. A building used to provide services of the company

3. A broken specialty chair that is not used in the business any longer

4. Employees

5. Money owed to the company from services provided

6. Money owed by the company to the bank

7. The land that the company's building is on

8. A vehicle owned by the company which is used to pick up patients and supplies

9. Money in the personal bank account of the owner

10. Money paid in advance for new equipment

Answers are provided at the end of this chapter.

Short-term Assets

Assets are normally sub-divided on the Balance Sheet into two categories. The first is called Short-term Assets (or current assets). These items will be used or converted into cash within a period of one year or less.

Long-term Assets

Long-term assets (also called non-current assets) are not expected to be converted to cash or totally "used up" in a year or less. Rather, they are expected to be of value to the company for more than a year. Long-term assets would include equipment, land, and buildings.

Intangible Assets

Intangible assets are assets that cannot be physically touched. They must still meet the three tests mentioned earlier in order to be listed on the Balance Sheet as an asset; however, they do not have any tangible characteristics. Some examples of intangible assets include trademarks, copyrights, patents, as long as they have been purchased from the prior owner of the business. You might be inclined to call goodwill an intangible asset; goodwill is based on location of the business, reputation of the owners and name recognition by the public, and is of great value to a business. Keep in mind, though, that because of the generally accepted accounting principles discussed in Chapter 2, this and any valuable item which was not paid for, and thus does not have a historical cost, cannot be listed on the balance sheet as an asset.

Liabilities

Refer to the Balance Sheet of Desert Medical Care Company above. The total liabilities of the business are equal to $221,000. As with the assets, the liabilities list represents both short-term and long-term items. Again, similar to the list of assets, the short-term liabilities will be paid off in a period not to exceed one year. The long-term liabilities will remain as debt to the company for longer than one year.

With this or any long-term debt, a portion of it becomes due and payable each year. Thus, most companies' Balance Sheets show the current portion of all long-term debt separately, in the short-term liabilities section.

Owner's Equity

As we have discussed above, the equity of Desert Medical Care Company comes from two sources. The Owner's Investment of $120,000 represents the amount invested in the business by the owner through the purchase of various assets or as money in the bank that is meant for the business. The retained earnings of a negative $21,000 represent the amount of loss incurred by the business since its inception.

↪Alert

Understanding Cash and Retained Earnings: Let's take a moment to clarify a very important point about retained earnings that often causes confusion among owners of small and large businesses alike. The retained earnings in a business are not equal to cash, that is, "money in the bank." Just because a company has kept profits in the business over the years does not mean that all of these profits have been retained in the form of cash. For example, after the company earns a profit, it may take that cash and purchase assets or pay off some of its liabilities. Business owners often assume that they are doing well because they are making profits without taking into account the amount of cash they have at their disposal. If they do not have sufficient cash, however, they will find themselves in dire straits since they may not be able to make the payroll, pay their taxes, or pay for other liabilities. It is absolutely essential that businesses have a good cash management plan.

A revised balance sheet for Desert Medical Care Company using the most common sub-headings would look like the one shown in Figure 3.4.

Figure 3.4

The Expanded Balance Sheet

DESERT MEDICAL CARE COMPANY
Balance Sheet
January 3, 2011

Assets

Short-Term Assets:
Cash..........................$9,050

Money Market Acct..........50,000
Supplies.......................60,950
Total Short-Term Assets...120,000

Long-Term Assets
Computers.................$45,000
Med. Software..............45,000
Furniture & Equipment....100,000
Security Deposit.............10,000

Total Long-Term Asset........$200,000

Total Assets.............$320,000

Liabilities & Owner's Equity

Short-Term Liabilities
Current Portion of
Bank Loan...................$20,000
Taxes Payable.................6,000
Salaries Payable 5,000
Total Short-Term
Liabilities....................31,000
Long-term Liabilities:
Bank Loan...................180,000
Retirement Payable..........10,000
Total Long-Term
Total Liabilities...........$221,000
Owner's Equity:
Owner's Investment......$120,000
Retained Earnings.......... (21,000)
Total Owner's Equity.........$99,000

**Total Liabilities and
Owner's Equity.........$320,000**

The Transactions Behind the Balance Sheet

Referring to the Balance Sheet in Figure 3.4, let's examine the transactions that created it.

Dr. Sarah Invests Money in the Company (Owner's Investment)

First, let's assume that on January 1, 2011, the Dr. Sarah invests $120,000 in her medical care company. In other words, she takes $120,000 out of her personal bank account and sets up a new account with the bank for the new business. After this transaction, the company's balance sheet looks like the one presented in Figure 3.5:

Figure 3.5

DESERT MEDICAL CARE COMPANY
Balance Sheet
January 1, 2011

Assets	Liabilities & Owner's Equity
Short-Term Assets:	Liabilities.............................…...$0
Cash...................$120,000	*Owner's Equity::*
	Owner's Investment….…....$120,000
Total Assets...........**$120,000**	**Total Liabilities and Owner's Equity**.............**$120,000**

On the Balance Sheet the cash and owner's investment are increased by $120,000. Note that the balance sheet continues to balance, i.e. assets = liabilities + owner's equity.

Dr. Sarah Purchases Computers, Electronic Medical Records Software, and Equipment (Long-Term Assets)

Next, on January 1, the medical care company buys computers, Electronic Medical Records Software and Furniture and Equipment. The Computers have a value of $45,000, the software is $45,000 and the Furniture and Equipment is $100,000. All of these values are the actual amounts that the Company pays. Because the company does not have sufficient cash to pay for all of these assets at the current time, it decides to borrow some money. It pays $65,000 in cash for these assets and takes out a bank loan for $200,000 to purchase supplies and pay for the security deposit and have some additional cash. This is a 10-year loan. $20,000 of this loan is due and payable within one year and each year thereafter plus interest of 6% payable on the outstanding balance of the loan. After these transactions, the company's Balance Sheet looks like the one presented in Figure 3.6:

Figure 3.6
DESERT MEDICAL CARE COMPANY
Balance Sheet
January 1, 2011

Assets	Liabilities & Owner's Equity
Short-Term Assets:	*Liabilities:*
Short-term:	Short term:
	Current Portion of Mort.
Cash..............................$130,000	Payable.........................$20,000
Total Short-Term Assets......$130,000	
	Total Liabilities.............$200,000
Long-Term Assets	
Computers.......................$45,000	*Owner's Equity:*
Software..........................$45,000	Owner's Investment..........$120,000
Furniture & Equipment.......$100,000	
Total Long-Term Assets.....$190,000	
	Total Liabilities and
Total Assets................$320,000	**Owner's Equity............$320,000**

As you can see in Figure 3.6 the cash balance has decreased by $65,000 (the amount of cash spent to the purchase of the Computers, Software, and Furniture and Equipment), the other assets have increased to $190,000 (the Computers, Software, and Furniture and Equipment), and two new liabilities have appeared (the current and long-term portions of the bank loan). The loan of $200,000 has been divided up between the short-term portion of $20,000 and the long-term portion (due in a period of greater than one year) of $180,000. Since the company borrowed $200,000, and only needed $125,000 to pay for these assets, the remaining $75,000 was added to cash, giving us a total in cash of $130,000 (Beginning of $120,000 - $65,000, +$75,000)

Also, notice that the owner's equity is not affected.

What are the factors that change Owner's Equity? The items below give us a summary of the ONLY items that have an impact on the beginning balance of Owner's Equity.

• The owner invests more money in the business

• The business makes a profit or loss

• The owner takes assets out of the business.

Thus, when Dr. Sarah invested the $120,000 into the Medical Care Company, this increased her owner's equity in the company by this same amount. When the company makes a profit, this is also an increase to her owner's equity. Finally, if Dr. Sarah decides to take any money or other assets out of the Medical Care Company for her own use, this will reduce the owner's equity as it shows up on the Medical Care Company's balance sheet.

Dr. Sarah Purchases supplies (Short-Term Asset)

On January 3, the company purchases supplies. The cost of these supplies is $60,950. . After this transaction, the Balance Sheet looks like it does in Figure 3.7:

Figure 3.7

DESERT MEDICAL CARE COMPANY
Balance Sheet
January 3, 2011

Assets   **Liabilities & Owner's Equity**

Short-Term Assets: *Liabilities:*

Short-term: Short Term:

Cash...........................$69,050   Current Portion of
                                               Bank Loan.................$20,000
Supplies.......................60,950
                                               Long-term:
Total Short-Term Assets...$130,000   Bank Loan.................180,000

                                               Total Liabilities.........$200,000

Long-Term Assets   *Owner's Equity:*

Computers...................$45,000   Owner's Investments.....$120,000

Med. Software................45,000

Furniture & Equipment.....100,000

Total Long-Term Assets...$190,000

                                               Total Liabilities and
Total Assets..............$320,000   **Owner's Equity........$320,000**

In Figure 3.7 the only change in the balance sheet after the purchase of the supplies, where there has been an exchange of one asset (cash) for another asset (supplies) for the exact amount of $50,950.

Dr. Sarah Invests Cash into a Money Market Account (Short-Term Asset).

On January 10, the company invests part of its excess cash into a Money Market Account.. The investment is for $50,000. . After this transaction, the Balance Sheet looks like it does in Figure 3.8:

Figure 3.8

DESERT MEDICAL CARE COMPANY
Balance Sheet
January 3, 2011

Assets	Liabilities:
Short-Term Assets:	Current Portion of Bank Loan...........$20,000
Short-term:	Long-term:
Cash..................$19,050	Bank Loan.............180,000
Money Market Acct........50,000	Total
Supplies................60,950	Liabilities............$200,000
Total Short-Term Assets.$130,000	*Owner's Equity:*
Long-Term Assets	Owner's Investment.......$120,000
Computers...............$45,000	
Med. Software...........45,000	
Furniture & Equipment....100,000	
Total Long-Term Assets.$190,000	
Total Assets............$320,000	**Total Liabilities and Owner's Equity........$320,000**

In Figure 3.8 the only change in the balance sheet where there has been an exchange of one asset (cash) for another asset (money market account) for the exact amount of $50,000.

Dr. Sarah Must Pay a Security Deposit.

The landlord of the premises where Dr. Sarah has her medical practice has requested a security deposit of $10,000 on January 5. This money will be returned to Dr. Sarah upon the conclusion of the rental agreement or when she leaves the premises. In Figure 3.9, the results of this transaction would change the Balance Sheet in the following manner:

Figure 3.9

DESERT MEDICAL CARE COMPANY
Balance Sheet
January 5, 2011

Assets	Liabilities & Owner's Equity
Short-Term Assets:	*Liabilities:*
Short-term:	
Cash..........................$9,050	Current Portion of Bank Loan...$20,000
Money Market Acct...............50,000	Long-term:
Supplies...........................60,950	Bank Loan.........................180,000
Total Short-Term Assets....$130,000	**Total Liabilities..........$200,000**
Long-Term Assets	*Owner's Equity:*
Computers......................$45,000	Owner's Investment............$120,000
Med. Software....................45,000	
Furniture & Equipment.........100,000	
Security Deposit..................10,000	
Total Long-Term Assets.......$190,000	**Total Liabilities and**
Total Assets.................$320,000	**Owner's Equity..............$320,000**

Thus, the only change in the Balance Sheet is that a short-term asset (cash) has been turned into a long-term asset (Deposit) for $10,000.

> **Note:** *This Balance Sheet represented in Figure 3.9 is not the same as the ones in Figures 3.2 and 3.4, because those are for one full year, and this represents the assets, liabilities and owner's equity as of January 5, 2011.*

In this Chapter, you have learned about the Balance Sheet and the definitions of all of its components. You have learned how these components relate to each other. You have also learned a very important point: retained earnings are not necessarily comprised of only cash, and therefore, cash management is a high priority to a business making a profit. Finally, you learned how various transactions affect the Balance Sheet of a small business.

Answers to Quiz

1. No. This would not appear on the company's balance sheet, since this is an asset that belongs to the owner and not the business.

2. Yes, because this asset is used by the business.

3. No. This was once an asset, but is no longer one since it is not used in the operations of the business.

4. No. Although a company's employees are often referred to as "assets," they are not listed as assets on a company's balance sheet since the company does not own them.

5. Yes. This is called accounts receivable.

6. No. This is a liability, not an asset (something owed rather than something owned.).

7. This depends on whether the company owns the land. If it does, the land is considered an asset because it has value.

8. Yes.

9. No. This is an asset of the owner not of the company, and these assets are kept separate.

10. Yes, this has future benefit to the company since the insurance company owes them insurance for three years into the future.

Glossary

Accounting Equation: A(ssets) = L(iabilities) + OE (Owner's Equity), The formula depicts the relationships of the various elements of the balance sheet to each other.

Accounts Payable: A short-term liability (debt) incurred from the purchase of inventory or other short-term assets.

Assets: Items of value that are owned by the company and are represented on the balance sheet. In order for an item to be shown on the balance sheet, it must meet three tests; 1) the company must control it or own it, 2) the item must have some value to the company and 3) this value must be measurable. Assets are categorized as short-term or long-term items.

Balance Sheet: This financial statement is a listing of the assets (items owned), liabilities (items owed) and owner's equity (what belongs to the owner(s)). The relationships between all these items are represented by the accounting equation.

Creditors: Those individuals or companies to which money or other assets are owed, for example, the supplier from whom Dr. Sarah purchased the supplies.

Equity: See Owner's Equity

Historical Cost: The amount paid for an item owned by the business (assets) , or the amount incurred in a debt on the date of the agreement to enter into the obligation (liabilities). Even though over time the values of these assets and/or liabilities may change, they will always be shown on the balance sheet at their historical cost.

Intangible Assets: Those assets that are of value to a business and meet all tests of being an asset, but do not have tangible qualities, for example trademarks and patents.

Liabilities: Debts owed by a business. They can either be short-term or long-term depending upon when they become due. Short-term liabilities are to be paid within a year. Examples in the Medical Care Company are the accounts payable, and the current portion of the mortgage payable. Long-term liabilities extend beyond one year. An example in the medical care company is the bank loan which is due to be paid beyond the current year.

Long-Term Assets: Those items that will be consumed or converted to cash after a period of one year. Examples of these assets in the medical company are the computers, the software and the EQUIPMENT

Owner's Equity: The difference between what is owned and what is owed; in a company, this amount belongs to the owners. The owner's equity is made up of the original and additional investments by the owner, plus any profit that is retained in the business minus any cash or other assets that are withdrawn or distributed to the owner(s).

Retained Earnings: The amount of profit earned by the business since its inception minus any money that is taken out or distributed to the owner(s). At the medical care company, this is whatever Dr. Sarah earns in selling her services minus whatever expenses she incurs, for example, electricity, rent, bank loan interest payments, salaries, etc.

Short-term assets: Those assets that are cash or will be converted to cash or consumed within a period of one year or less. Examples of these assets in the medical care company are cash, money market accounts, the security deposit and supplies.

Chapter 4

The Income Statement

This chapter covers the following information:

✓ Understanding the Income Statement

✓ The Income Statement Illustrated

✓ Transactions That Affect the Income Statement

At this point, we are familiar with the balance sheet and how it is helpful in showing what assets Desert Medical Care Company owns and what liabilities the company owes. We also learned that the difference between these two items is called owner's equity and represents what the medical practice is "worth" at the end of the year. The final thing that we learned was that the balance sheet represents these values for one particular point in time and for that point in time only. It can be considered a snapshot of the business.

Now that her business is up and running, Dr. Sarah is very interested in knowing, 'What is the bottom line? How much money did I make?" For this information Dr. Sarah should become familiar with the Income Statement.

Understanding the Income Statement

The Income Statement presents a summary of an entity's revenues (the money coming in) and expenses (the money going out to generate revenue) for a specific period of time, such as a month, a quarter or a year. This period of time is known as the accounting period. One key difference between the Income Statement and the Balance Sheet is that the Income Statement reflects a period of time rather than a single moment in time as with the Balance Sheet. The Income Statement is also called a Statement of Earnings or a Statement of Operations.

The preparation of the Income Statement serves several purposes. Often, the only reason one uses the Income Statement is to concentrate on the "bottom line" or net income (revenue minus expenses). The Income Statement can also be useful for analyzing changes in the revenue data over a period of time, or determining ratios of particular expenses to revenue and how these ratios have been changing over certain periods of time. These two topics will be discussed in Chapter 8 and 9.

The Income Statement Illustrated

In Figure 4.1 we can see all of Desert Medical Care Company revenue and expenses for her first year in business. By reviewing these numbers Dr. Sarah can also see her "bottom line," that is, her net income for the year.

In general, income statements are organized into three sections. The first section shows the revenues earned from services for the period being reported. In the case of the Desert Medical Care Company (Figure 4.1) this period is one year. The second section lists the expenses the business has incurred to earn these revenues during the period represented by the income statement. The third section is the difference between these revenues and expenses, in which we hope the revenues outweigh the expenses, indicating a profit. If the expenses are greater than the revenues, this would indicate a loss – not something sustainable over the long term in a business.

In the example below, the numbers listed inside of parentheses represent subtractions.

Figure 4.1

DESERT MEDICAL CARE COMPANY
Income Statement
For the Year Ended December 31, 2011

Income..$129,000

Operating Expenses:

Salaries of Employees...............$50,000

Office Expenses

(Phone, Supplies, etc)................20,000

Insurance Expense...................18,000

Rent and Utilities....................25,000

Repayment of Loan..................20,000

Continuing Education & Meetings...5,000

Total Operating Expenses.....................138,000

Net Income from Operations....................(9,000)

Other Revenue and Expenses:

Interest Expense (6% on $200,000)................(12,000)

Net Loss before Taxes..............................($21,000)

Less: Income Taxes ....–0-

Net Loss...($21,000)

Alert

Frequently in the first year of a medical practice, the medical professional will not have any profits, but rather there will be a net loss. This is normally caused by the initial investments that have to be made, as well as a period needed to develop the medical practice business.

Modified Cash Basis Accounting

Most medical practices choose to use modified cash basis accounting because it more realistically reflects the status of their medical practice. Income or revenue is recognized when the money is received, not when it is billed (or earned). Due to the vicissitudes of insurance billing, a medical practitioner can bill, for example, $100,000 to medical insurance companies, and expect to receive less than half that amount in income. Using the accrual accounting concept, all that billing would be recognized as revenue – this would create an unrealistic expectation of profitability of the medical practice and may induce the medical practitioner to make investments in equipment or other purchases which would not be a prudent use of cash. In modified cash basis accounting, liabilities are recognized when they are incurred, not when they are paid. Therefore, when a medical practitioner purchases, on credit, equipment or supplies, those purchases are recognized on the balance sheet as liabilities before a check is written to pay for the purchase. (When the payment is made, cash is reduced and the liability is reduced or eliminated). Using this method of accounting more accurately reflects the true profitability of the medical practice. Many accountants are not familiar with the modified cash basis because they are so accustomed to the accrual basis of accounting used by most businesses. Clearly, medical practices have different needs and the modified cash basis accounting fills one of those needs – to have and understand the status of their medical practice business.

↪Alert

Medical practice owners starting a medical business would be well advised to select an accountant familiar with modified cash basis accounting.

The Accrual Concept

The Accrual Concept addresses the issue of when revenue is recognized on the income statement. Revenue is recognized when it is earned and expenses are recognized as they are incurred regardless of when the cash changes hands; this is referred to as accrual basis of accounting. This type of accounting is used by most businesses throughout the United States for the presentation of their financial statements. Some small firms, including most medical practices as well as most individuals still use the modified cash basis of accounting to determine their income and income taxes. Under the modified cash basis of accounting, revenue is not reported until cash is received, and expenses are reported when they are incurred.

Generally Accepted Accounting Principles and Accrual Accounting

Because GAAP (generally accepted accounting principles) requires the accrual system of accounting, and most financial statements that you will encounter used by bankers and investors will be prepared under the accrual system of accounting, we will use the accrual basis of accounting for all of our examples.

Revenue

Revenue is the total amount of money obtained during a particular period of time by a business, or individual, from the rendering of medical services to patients. Additional revenue can be earned from sales of products, interest, or dividends or any combination of these. The sum of all of these sources is the total revenues of the business.

As shown in Figure 4.1 revenue of $129,000 is from the medical services provided to patients.

At this point there has been no discussion of net income. Revenue is one component of net income, but it is not the whole story. Expenses and other items need to be added to or subtracted from revenue to arrive at the net income figure.

➥Alert

Revenue versus Cash Flow: It is important to note that revenue is not equal to cash flow. Revenue can be generated prior to a business receiving cash. In other words, a sale can be made or services rendered where only a promise to pay is generated, but cash does not change hands. Even though the cash will not be collected until some point in the future, the revenue is recognized at the time that the merchandise has been transferred to the buyer, or the seller has performed the services. Therefore, it is possible for a company to have a large amount of sales (or revenue) and still have a cash flow problem, since they have not collected the money yet. In medical practices, the business will only collect a portion of the billings for services.

In Figure 4.1, we can see that collecting cash for Dr. Sarah's services generated the $129,000 of revenue.

Expenses

Expenses represent the cost of doing business. Examples of expenses are rent, utilities, bank service fees, tool and equipment expenses, bad debt expense, and salaries. In our current example, the expenses of Desert Medical Care Company fall under the title of Operating Expenses. These are all of the expenses for the year 2011 that were incurred by the company in order to generate revenue in the operation of the business. The total is $138,000.

There is an important distinction to be made between an expenditure and an expense. An expenditure is the spending of cash. All expenses are expenditures; however, not all expenditures are expenses. It sounds confusing, but it's really quite simple. An expense is an expenditure that generates revenue. If the expenditure does not immediately generate revenue, it is not an expense. Consider the purchase of a building. When the purchase of a building is made it does not immediately produce revenue. At that point in time the purchase is considered an expenditure. However, over time this building will be used in the production of revenue, and the building (and other such long-term assets) depreciate or are used up. The depreciation of the building thus becomes an expense and is matched with those revenues it helped to generate.

Net Income

Net income represents the difference between revenues generated during the period and the related expenses which generated that revenue.

Once again note that the term cash is not used. As with revenue, part of the "bottom line" or net income could be made up of cash, but other parts could be made up of promises to receive cash or promises to pay cash in the future.

☞ Quick Tip:

Expand Your Focus: When evaluating your business, you should not only concentrate on net income in the financial statements. This is certainly a useful number (especially if it is compared to previous years' figures), but there are several other important numbers and ratios that ultimately might be important to your decisions. Some of these numbers might include gross income, the trend of salary expenses (Are they going up too fast?), how much cash is on hand at the end of the year, how sales have been increasing, if at all. Outside of the company it is important to pay attention to the competition as well as the economy as a whole. These are just a few examples of why if you only focus on the net income figure, you will lose sight of the whole picture.

In Figure 4.1, the term "net loss" appears three times. The first time is "Net Loss From Operations". This number, $9,000 represents the income loss from providing services, the main purpose of Desert Medical Care Company.

Then the company had other interest expenses of $12,000. This is subtracted from Net Loss (or Net Income), yielding Net Income Before Taxes. If there had been a Net Income, taxes would be due and payable, and would be subtracted from Net Income Before Taxes, yielding a different number for Net Income. Since during this first year of business, Dr. Sarah's business did not make any income, there are no taxes due, thus the number of Net Income Before Taxes is the same as Net Income. Thus, the bottom line is a Net Loss of $21,000.

Confusing? Maybe a little, but accounting convention requires that we separate out net income from the main operations of the business and from other income earned from other types of sales and services. After these two numbers are shown separately on the income statement, we have to show what the government is going to take in taxes before we can finally arrive at the "bottom line."

Interest and Income Taxes

Other items subtracted from revenues and expenses before determining the total net income are interest and income taxes. Most accountants classify interest and taxes as an "other expense" of the period, not as an operating expense. The reason for this is that interest and taxes do not produce mainstream revenue, but are necessary to pay in order to stay in business.

Quiz

Based upon your knowledge of accounting so far, looking at the Income Statement in Figure 4.1, would you say that the Desert Medical Care Company had a good first year of business? What would you like to see the medical business do differently next year? What additional information do you need to make these decisions?

Answers appear at the end of this chapter.

Transactions That Affect the Income Statement

Let's examine the transactions that created the Income Statement in Figure 4.1.

Income

In the revenue section above we looked at the total revenue (or income) for the year. Now let's look at an individual income during the year, and see what effect it has on the Income Statement. What we have been looking at in Figure 4.1 is the income statement at the end of the year. Now let's go back to the beginning of the year and see how these final figures in Figure 4.1 were derived.

Assume that on January 6, the company's first patient service resulted in a total billing of $500. After this transaction the Income Statement would look like the one in Figure 4.2. (Note that this Income Statement in Figure 4.2 is as of January 6, whereas the one in Figure 4.1, is as of December 31.)

Figure 4.2

DESERT MEDICAL CARE COMPANY

Income Statement
For the Week Ended January 6, 2011

Revenue $500

Expenses . . . . – 0 –

Net Income $500

This transaction has caused a change to the Income Statement. It has increased the revenue account called "Revenue" by $500. At the same time this transaction has changed the Balance Sheet in several ways. Assuming that these services were provided for cash, the asset account (cash) on the Balance Sheet would increase by $500. The other change on the Balance Sheet is that the retained earnings figure goes up by the same $500. (Note: Remember that revenue minus expenses equals net income, and net income increases Retained Earnings on the Balance Sheet.

Now let's look at the Accounting Equation, A = L + OE that we learned about in Chapter 1. One asset, cash, has increased by the amount of the services provided of $500. Retained earnings, part of owner's equity, has increased by the same $500. Thus the left side of this equation has increased by $500 (Cash up by $500) and the right side of the equation, owner's equity, has increased by the same amount, $500.

Using the equation, the transaction would look like this:

Assets = Liabilities + Owner's Equity

Cash + $500   Net Income +$500

This concept is further demonstrated in Chapter 6, "Recording Transactions in the Double Entry Accounting System."

Operating Expenses

Operating expenses are those costs that are necessary to operate the business on a day-to-day basis. On January 7, Desert Medical Care Company pays the employees their first week's pay of $1000.

After this, second transaction the Income Statement looks like the one in Figure 4.3:

Figure 4.3

DESERT MEDICAL CARE COMPANY
Income Statement
For the Week Ended January 7, 2011

Revenue $500

Expenses 1000

Net Loss................................ ($ 500)

The $1000 paid to the employees is an expense (Salary Expense) and as such it is shown in the Income Statement under expenses. The net income is decreased by the entire $1000, as is the retained earnings and the cash in the Balance Sheet. Assuming that the salary is paid in cash, the impact on the accounting equation would look like this:

Assets = Liabilities + Owner's Equity

Cash - $1000   Net Income - $1000

Besides the payment of salaries to her employees, Dr. Sarah incurred various other operating expenses as can be seen in Figure 4.1. These included Office Expenses, Insurance Expense, Rent and Utilities, a partial Repayment of the 10-year loan, and Continuing Education and Meetings. All of these expenses are handled exactly the same as in the example above with the payment of salaries; that is an increase in an expense (that reduces net income and subsequently Owner's Equity) and also a reduction in cash. The transaction would look like this:

Cash -$XX   Net Income -$XX

Other Revenue and Expenses

During the year, Desert Medical Care Company incurred other expenses that were necessary to operate the business. The business had to pay interest on the mortgage that it held. Since the mortgage is for $200,000, and the interest rate on this loan is 6%, the total interest paid during the year is $12,000. If Dr. Sarah had earned any other revenue that was not directly related to her main business, such as selling other products in her office to her patients, this would be recorded here under Other Revenue and Expenses.

In this Chapter you learned the components of an Income Statement and how they relate to each other. You also learned that revenue and net income are not the same as cash. Finally, you learned how individual transactions affect and change the Income Statement.

In Chapter 5 you will find out how to prepare and use a Statement of Cash Flows.

ANSWER TO QUIZ

It is not possible to make a complete analysis of a company just by looking at one financial statement. Dr. Sarah, the owner, and we as outsiders would also need to look at the balance sheet as well as the statement of cash flows (to be discussed in the next Chapter).

It is important to note that the Desert Medical Care Company did not make a profit during this first year. Many new, small businesses do not make a profit for the first two or three years, so this is a normal thing.

In planning for the year ahead, Dr. Sarah might decide to put more money into marketing in order to expand her business. Other information it would be helpful to examine would be other financial statements as well as the budgets for the next two years, 2011 and 2012.

Glossary

Accrual Basis of Accounting: This accounting method recognizes transactions when revenue is earned, expenses are incurred, and purchases take place–whether or not cash changes hands at that moment. This is the method of accounting used by virtue of generally accepted accounting principle, and most businesses use this rather than the alternative, the modified cash basis of accounting. However, medical practices predominately use the modified cash basis of accounting because it provides more realistic information on net profit. Medical practices, by not recognizing income or revenue until money is received, don't count their chickens before they hatch.

Bottom Line: Another term used for Net Income, it represents all expenses subtracted from all revenues. This figure gets its name from the fact that it appears at the bottom of the income statement.

Cash Basis of Accounting: This accounting method only recognizes revenue and expenses when cash is exchanged. If the sale or expense takes place in one period without cash changing hands, because of receivables and payables, the revenue and the expenses are not recognized until a future period. For this reason, the cash basis of accounting is typically not used for business according to GAAP, but is the method generally used in personal accounting.

Modified Cash Basis Accounting: Revenue or income is recognized only when cash is received, but liabilities are recognized when they are incurred. Thus, accounts payable are recognized as an expense even though no cash has yet been used to pay for the item. This is the most common form of accounting used in small medical practices in the U.S.

Expenditures: The spending of cash. All expenses are expenditures, however all expenditures are not expenses. Only expenditures which immediately generate revenue are considered expenses. When expenditures are made for items that have future benefits, they are classified as assets and converted to expenses as they are used up. An example of such an asset would be an electrocardiogram machine with a lifespan of several years. Expenditures over a certain amount (determined by the IRS) must be "capitalized" and the cost spread over a period of time. This is called depreciation. This concept causes confusion in the minds of many medical practitioners because cash is used to pay for the capital equipment, but the equipment is only recognized as an expense over a period of time.

Expenses: Expenses are expenditures made to generate revenue. Whether or not cash changes hands, a company incurs an expense as soon as it makes a commitment to pay for a product or service.

Income Statement: This financial statement is a listing of all revenues and expenses of the business earned or incurred during a particular period of time. A company usually produces the income statement monthly, quarterly, or annually. It is one of the three major statements produced by businesses in the United States, the other two being the balance sheet and the statement of cash flows.

Net income: The difference between revenue and expenses for a designated period of time. In the case of Desert Medical Care Company we saw three uses of the term net income. The first, net income from operations shows all normal revenue and expenses that deal with the main operations of this business. The second usage was net income before taxes, where net income from operations is increased and reduced by other revenue and expenses that are outside the normal operations of this business. The third usage was net income. This is what is referred to as the "bottom line" since it appears at the bottom of the income statement. It has been derived by reducing net income before taxes, by the amount of income taxes for the year.

Recognize: This term refers to the recording of the revenues and expenses in the records of the company. This occurs at the point in time when revenue and expenses are shown on the income statement. In most medical practices, revenues are recognized when cash or payment is received for services rendered. Expenses are recognized when they are incurred and become an obligation of the medical practice.

Revenue: The amount earned by a business by selling goods or performing services is termed "revenue." In the case of the Desert Medical Care Company, revenue represents the money brought in from providing medical services.

Chapter 5

Preparing and Using A Statement Of Cash Flows

This chapter covers the following information:

✓ What is a Statement of Cash Flows?

✓ Cash and Cash Equivalents

✓ The Statement of Cash Flows Illustrated

After analyzing the balance sheet and the income statement for Desert Medical Care Company, Dr. Sarah had a clear understanding of what she owned and what she owed, as well as what her "bottom line" was for the year. Although things are looking good so far, Dr. Sarah has a nagging concern which she raises at a meeting with her business advisor: "I have read that many small businesses go bankrupt, not because they don't have a great product or a great service, but because they run out of cash. Is that right?"

Well, Dr. Sarah is right. As we discussed in Chapter 4, making a profit, or having a large amount in Retained Earnings, does not equal having cash. And if there is no cash, there is no way to pay the salaries, pay the IRS, or pay any other bills for that matter. In this chapter we will discuss the Statement of Cash Flows, the financial statement which will help Sarah in her quest to stay on top of the cash flow in her business.

What Is A Statement of Cash Flows?

For a company's financial statement to be in accordance with
Generally Accepted Accounting Principles (GAAP), the Statement of
Cash Flows must be included as one of the four required financial
statements. Do you remember the other three? They are the Balance
Sheet, The Income Statement, and Statement of Retained Earnings.

The Statement of Cash Flows shows the flow of cash within the
business –where the cash came from and how it was spent during the
period of reporting (which is generally a month, a quarter, or a year). It
also shows the cash flows of the company divided into categories
according to three major activities: operating, investing, and financing.
This is helpful to statement users, business owners, investors, and
creditors because it indicates the type of transaction that gave rise to
each one of the cash flows.

Additionally, the Statement of Cash Flows differs from the Balance
Sheet and Income Statement in two key ways. The Balance Sheet
shows the financial status of a company at the end of the reporting
period (a snapshot), but both the Income Statement and the Statement
of Cash Flows show the flow of activity during the reporting period (a
short movie compared to the snapshot that is the Balance Sheet). The
second difference is that the Income Statement reports this activity on
the modified cash accounting basis or accrual basis, and the Statement
of Cash Flows reports it on the cash basis. Remember from Chapter 4,
that under the modified cash basis of accounting, revenue is not
reported until cash is received, and expenses are reported when they
are incurred, rather than when cash is disbursed.

What is the Purpose of the Statement?

Like the other required financial statements you have learned about—
the Balance Sheet and the Income Statement--the Statement of Cash
Flows enables users to make decisions about the company. The
Statement of Cash Flows is more like the Income Statement than the
Balance Sheet in that it is a change statement. It shows the transactions
that caused cash levels to change from the beginning of the period to

the end. As was mentioned earlier, a company can make a profit or earn a large amount of revenue, but not have enough cash to pay its bills, so it is critically important to review both the "bottom line" as well as the company's position in cash to really forecast its future.

There are several ways in which you might use a Statement of Cash Flows in your own life. Will you have sufficient cash at the end of the month to purchase additional inventory? Will you have the cash flow in the future to buy the new equipment you'll need to handle all the growth you're experiencing? Will you have the cash necessary to purchase a new building for the planned expansion?

Cash and Cash Equivalents

In business, the term "cash" has a broader meaning than the amount of cash in the bank at the end of the year. It is also defined as liquid short-term investments; liquid investments are those which can quickly be converted into cash within a very short period of time, usually by cashing them in (in the case of certificates of deposit, for example) or by selling them.   For this reason, they are also referred to as cash equivalents. (See Figure 5.1 for examples.) Therefore whenever the term "cash" is used in this chapter it refers to cash and all cash equivalents.

Figure 5.1

Examples of Cash Equivalents

• Cash in the Bank

• Commercial Paper (a form of short-term loan)

• Any investment that has a maturity date of less than three months

• Certificates of Deposit

• Money Market Accounts

• U.S. Government Treasury Bills

The Statement of Cash Flows Illustrated

By looking at the Balance Sheet in Chapter 3, Figure 3.2, you can see how much cash the Desert Medical Care Company has at the end of 2011--$59,050 (When we include the Cash and the Money Market Account). By reviewing the Statement of Cash Flows in Figure 5.2 below, we can see where the cash came from and where it went during 2011.

Figure 5.2

DESERT MEDICAL CARE COMPANY
Statement of Cash Flows
For the Year Ended December 31, 2011

Note: Parentheses indicate decreases in cash

Cash Flow from Operating Activities:
Security Deposit..............................(10,000)
Supplies.....................................(60,950)
Total Cash Flow from Operations.....($70,950)

Cash Flow from Investing Activities:
Purchase of Computers.......................(45,000)
Purchase of Computer Software...............(45,000)
Purchase of Furniture & Equipment..........(100,000)
Total Cash Flow from
Investing Activities...............($190,000)

Cash Flow from Financing Activities:
Borrowing for the Mortgage....................$200,000
Owner's Investment............................ 120,000
Total Cash Flow from
Financing Activities.................$320,000
Net increase in Cash and
Cash Equivalents..................... $59,050

(Notice that this is the same number for ending cash on the Balance Sheet in Figure 3.2, if you combine Cash and the Money Market Account. Since there was no beginning balance in cash, 0 + this change = $59,050)

Now let's examine each of the statement's sections closely.

Operating Activities

As was mentioned earlier, the statement of cash flows reports cash flow related to three areas – operating activities, financial activities, and investment activities. This is because a list of cash flows means more to business owners, investors, and creditors as they analyze the business if they can determine the type of transaction that gave rise to each one of the cash flows.

Investing Activities

Any time a company makes a purchase of property, plant, or equipment, this addition is treated as an investment in the organization. This investment represents a cash flow FROM the company. Even though the entire purchase may not have been with cash, but with some borrowed money, the entire purchase is shown as a cash flow in the investing section of the cash flow statement, and any borrowing of money is shown separately in the financing section.

In Figure 5.2 we can see that the Desert Medical Care Company purchased three long-term assets during the year 2011. The computers for $45,000, the computer software also for $45,000, and the Equipment and Furniture for $100,000 are all shown as negative cash flows in the investing activities section of the cash flow statement. The total of these three purchases represents a negative cash flow from investing activities of $190,000.

Financing Activities

The section called financing activities represents the cash that has come into or out of the company for the purpose of financing all of the other activities of the business. This could include retained earnings and money brought in by stock issued by the company, or as we can see in Figure 5.2, the $120,000 that Dr. Sarah invested into the business on the first day. (Remember that Dr. Sarah's personal money is accounted for separately from the company's money. If she invests personal funds in the business, this may be a decrease in her personal cash funds, but it is an increase for the business.) Because this investment was in cash, it is shown as an increase in the cash flow from financing activities. In addition to this investment by Dr. Sarah, a 10-year loan was negotiated in order to purchase the three long-term assets: Computers, Computer Software and Equipment and Furniture. This loan for $200,000 is also shown as an inflow of cash to the business and thus an increase in cash flow from financing activities.

The total of these two items, $320,000, represents the total cash flow into the company from financing activities during the year 2011.

The total of the three cash flows--from operations, from investing and from financing--represents the total increase or decrease in cash and cash equivalents for the business during the year being reported (in this example, an increase of $59,050). Notice that this total represents the change in cash from the beginning of the year to the end of the year. In our example, cash at the beginning of the year was $0, and at the end was $59,050, a net increase.

In this Chapter you have learned how to prepare the Statement of Cash Flows. In Chapter 6 you will learn about the double-entry system of accounting and how transactions are recorded in the accounting books.

Glossary

The Statement of Cash Flows is one of the four required financial statements. This statement shows where the cash came from and how it was spent during the period of reporting.

Cash: Includes currency and coins, balances in checking accounts as well as any item that is acceptable into these checking accounts, such as checks and money orders.

Cash Equivalents: The cash held by a business as well as the liquid short-term investments that can quickly be converted into cash within a very short period of time.

Financing activities: One of the three categories of business activity represented on the Cash Flow Statement. This section of the statement represents the cash that has come into or out of the company for the purpose of financing all of the other activities. In the case of Desert Medical Care Company, this includes the money borrowed on the mortgage and the money invested in the business by Dr. Sarah.

Investing Activities: One of the three categories of business activity represented on the Cash Flow Statement. This section of the statement shows those purchases of property, plant, or equipment. These items are treated as an investment in the organization and represent a cash flow out of the company.

Operating Activities: One of the three categories of business activity represented on the Cash Flow Statement. This section of the statement shows how much cash was generated from operations, that is, the day-to-day running of the business. In the case of Desert Medical Care Company, this would include cash generated from the provision of medical services.

Chapter 6

The Corporation

This chapter covers the following information:

✓ Sole proprietorship and incorporation

✓ Types of corporations

✓ The Professional Corporations

✓ The advantages of incorporating a health care services business

The Professional Corporation (PC) differs significantly from a standard corporation. In a moment, we will first briefly discuss standard corporations and then describe professional corporations.

Up to this point we have been discussing Dr. Sarah's Desert Medical Care Company. This company has not been incorporated. Under law, Desert Medical Care Company is not a distinct "legal person", but rather, a wholly owned business entity known as a sole proprietorship. All the assets that Dr. Sarah owns and all the debts and liabilities she owes are hers personally.

For illustration, let's pretend Dr. Sarah's company is a bicycle shop, rather than a company supplying medical care services. Dr. Sarah could decide that she wants to expand her bicycle company using other peoples' money. She decides to incorporate and sell stock in her corporation. By forming a corporation, Dr. Sarah will be creating, under law, a separate legal entity. While businesses may be incorporated as nonprofit corporations, Dr. Sarah's bicycle company would not fall into the permissible types of nonprofit companies (charitable, educational, professional association, etc. – the so called 501(c) corporations). Dr. Sarah's corporation would be a for profit corporation.

Sole proprietorship and incorporation

When incorporating, the sole proprietor will lose the total control he or she had, and now be subject to state and federal laws governing corporations. For instance, a sole proprietor can just take money out of the cash account whenever the sole proprietor wishes. Of course, the sole proprietor will eventually need to pay taxes on the profit made in the business, but the profit is considered his or her money. A corporation has employees and stockholders. Dr. Sarah may take money out of her bicycle shop corporation as dividends. Distributed dividends become the personal income of Dr. Sarah and she'll need to pay taxes on them. Alternatively, Dr. Sarah could take money out of her bicycle corporation as a salaried employee. She will need to withhold Federal Income Tax and FICA at the time she takes salary. This is more trouble than simply taking money out of the cash account as she was able to do before she incorporated. One advantage of Dr. Sarah's incorporated bicycle company is that she can now sell stock and raise money to expand the business. The stock purchasers now become part owners of the corporation. In this scenario, Dr. Sarah may need to obtain permission from the Board (President, Secretary, Treasurer, and Board members) in order to issue dividends, and she'll need the Board's vote to set her salary.

Types of corporations

Corporations are granted limited liability under the law. This means that, with certain rare exceptions, creditors of a corporation can lay claim only to the assets of the corporation, and not to the personal assets of the owners (stockholders) of the corporation. Creditors of sole proprietorships, such as Dr. Sarah's bicycle company before she incorporated, can claim the personal assets of the individual(s) owning the business whenever the assets of the business entity are insufficient to satisfy the creditors' claims. Because of the corporate characteristic, states have laws that restrict the stockholders' right to withdraw all the assets from the corporation. These laws, for instance, prevent a corporation from paying dividends to stockholders whenever the net assets (assets minus liabilities) are at or below a certain level. This minimum net asset figure is often called the legal capital of the corporation.

In summary so far, a corporation becomes incorporated by registering it with one State's Secretary of State as a legal entity. The corporation protects the personal assets of the owners (stockholders) of the corporation against creditors' claims. The corporation can issue (sell) capital stock (ownership shares in the corporation) to others to raise money, and can issue dividends to stockholders, although the corporation is limited to distributing dividends only down to a certain net asset level in the corporation (the legal capital of the corporation). For a more complete discussion of corporations, see the book, Accounting for Non-Accountants, 2nd Edition by Wayne Label, CPA, Ph.D.

The Professional Corporation

Professional corporations are unique legal entities which differ substantially from standard (non-professional) corporations. Professional corporations (PCs) are incorporates under distinct statutes. Many states restrict the ownership of PCs to professionals licensed under other distinct statutes in state law. For instance, states commonly restrict PCs providing medical care services to licensed physicians. The purpose of such restrictions is to prohibit individuals who are not licensed physicians from directing the diagnosis and treatment of disease, which is the province of the physician.

When a professional corporation is formed (chartered or registered under state law with the State Secretary of State), capital stock is issued. This stock is owned by the physician owner(s). The assets of the corporation are owned by the stockholder, but unlike a standard corporation, the physician stockholder is not generally afforded personal asset protection for torts (civil legal wrongs) committed by the PC. When a physician obtains a bank loan to incorporate, the bank lending officer will insist that the physician owner of the capital stock of the PC personally guarantees the corporation's liability for the loan. That removes any possible claim by the physician that liability for the loan is limited to the corporation. If and when the physician is sued for medical malpractice, the physician is personally liable for any award or judgment made against the professional corporation. The plaintiff attorney generally will sue the physician's PC and the physician personally. There is no "corporate veil" protecting the physician from medical negligence lawsuit awards. The PC can issue dividends to the PC's stockholder(s), but these are, in general, limited by law to amounts that exceed a normal salary for a physician in that specialty.

Issuing PC corporate dividends may make sense when the income tax rate on dividends is less than the income tax rate of personal salary from the corporation.[1]

If the PC does not provide any personal liability protection, particularly from medical malpractice judgments or awards, and the owners of the PC cannot sell shares to non-professionals, such as non-physicians, what advantage is there in incorporating a medical practice? Almost all of the advantages are tax related. The corporation can write off all business related expenses. Medical insurance premiums, costs of business related travel, costs of continuing education, costs of professional liability insurance, and pension plan contributions are examples. Equipment can be purchased by the corporation and depreciated within the corporation.

The advantages of incorporating a health care services business

These advantages are substantial, resulting in most medical practices choosing to incorporate relatively soon after establishment of the business. Where previous PCs were limited to "C" corporations and "S" corporations (the difference being primarily the ability to retain income in the corporation for tax strategy purposes), now many states permit PCs to form Limited Liability Partnerships (LLPs) and incorporate as Limited Liability Companies (LLCs). LLCs are unique entities in that members (owners are called "members", not shareholders, in an LLC) have some limited protection from creditors where the debt is not related to the business of the LLC. Creditors of a member of an LLC are restricted to a "charging order", which is like a lien against distributions made by the LLC. While this charging order has some potential advantages in the non-PC form of an LLC, the holders of the charging order would encumber the money ("salary") distributed by the LLC to the debtor physician member, i.e., the charging order becomes effective only when there are distributions made from the LLC. LLPs and LLCs as professional legal entities have not yet had their limits tested in the cauldron of State Courts of

---

[1] Please note that throughout this book information provided is not legal advice and should not be inferred as legal advice. Readers should consult their own tax advisor for tax consulting and their own attorney for legal advice. The examples gives are for illustrative purposes only and may not apply in the particular jurisdiction of the reader.

Appeal and States' Supreme Courts. Decisions to incorporate a medical services business should be thoroughly discussed with legal counsel and your accountant before selecting the best form of incorporation for the individual(s) owner(s).

Dr. Sarah, after consultation with her accountant and a corporate attorney specializing in professional corporations, decides to establish a corporation, the Desert Medical Care Corporation, with Dr. Sarah as the corporate president, secretary, and treasurer. The corporation issues 1000 shares of capital stock at one dollar per share which Dr. Sarah purchases with one thousand dollars of her own money. Dr. Sarah chooses the "C" corporation entity.

Dr. Sarah can sell, give, or lease the assets of her previous company to the corporation. Her employee(s) now become the employees of the corporation. Because she can now expense the entire amount of medical insurance premiums for herself and for her employees, Dr. Sarah's corporation begins providing health insurance for herself and her employee(s). This benefit makes her employee(s) very happy. While Dr. Sarah would like to provide medical insurance to the children of her employee(s), Dr. Sarah determines, as a prudent corporate president, that the corporation cannot afford this additional expense. However, she makes known to the employee(s) that they can individually purchase this additional coverage.

Dr. Sarah has entered the business world as the owner of her own professional corporation. This corporation is subject to all State and Federal laws governing professional corporations. Dr. Sarah must realize that she cannot just remove money from the bank account as she wishes. She must take salary and pay federal income taxes on the salary as well as FICA taxes on salary, and must do so within a specified period of time. From now on, the corporation will likely be the entity purchasing or leasing equipment. In addition to Dr. Sarah's prodigious talents as a skilled physician, she must now become a corporate business executive. More important than ever, she must understand the accounting documents provided by her corporate accountant.

In this chapter you have learned the difference between a proprietorship and a corporation. A professional corporation has been discussed as well as the difference between a professional corporations and other types of corporations. Further, you have learned the pros and cons to forming a professional corporation.

In Chapter 7 you will learn about Double Entry Accounting, including: the general journal, the general ledger, adjusting journal entries, and closing journal entries.

Glossary

LLC is a limited liability company wherein there are "members" rather than stockholders, and a managing member who directs the LLC. Recently, more and more states are permitting health care corporations to exist in this format. There are some theoretical asset protection benefits of conducting a health care business in this format.

LLP is a limited liability partnership where partners' assets are not available to creditors. LLPs are a superior form of business entity than a general partnership. Not all states permit health care entities to operate as an LLP.

Professional corporations are unique legal entities but differ substantially from standard non-professional corporations. Professional corporations (PCs) are incorporated under distinct state statutes. Many states restrict the ownership of PCs to distinct health care professionals licensed under a particular state statute.

Sole Proprietorship is an unincorporated business owned by one person only.

Chapter 7

Double-Entry Accounting

This chapter covers the following information:

✓ The General Journal

✓ The General Ledger

✓ Adjusting Journal Entries

✓ Closing Journal Entries

The terms "debit" and "credit" are enough to induce fear in even the most intrepid non-accountant. But even though you may never become an accountant, you will need to understand these concepts in order to have a solid grasp of accounting and business. In this chapter you'll learn what these terms mean and how they are used in the world of accounting.

↪ Alert

What Is a Debit? The word debit simply refers to the left side of the amount columns and the word credit identifies the right side of the amount columns. Nothing more, nothing less. Debit does not mean something unfavorable and credit does not mean something favorable, as some non-accountants often believe.

The General Journal

Sometime after a business transaction occurs it is recorded in a book called the general journal. While there are many different kinds of journals, it is most important to focus on the general journal. A general journal is often referred to as the book of original entry because this journal is the book in which a transaction is first recorded.

The pages of a general journal will look something like the one shown below in Figure 7.1 (The entries in this figure do not come from Desert Medical Care Company, but are simply examples):

Figure 7.1

Journal

				Amounts
Date	**Entries**	**Reference**	**Debits**	**Credits**
01/05/10	Land	Bought land for cash	20,000	
	Cash			20,000
01/31/10	Salary Expense	Paid Salary for the month of January with cash	4,000	
	Cash			4,000

Journal Entries

To illustrate how transactions are recorded in the general journal you can use the transactions described in Chapters 3 and 4. But first let's go back to the Accounting Equation we talked about in Chapter 1.

$$A = L + OE$$

The standard accounting rule is that assets, or the left side of the equation, are increased with debits, and decreased with credits, while the right side of the equation, the liabilities and the owner's equity items are just the opposite, that is they are increased with credits, and decreased with debits. When you increase or decrease the debits, by the same amount as you increase or decrease the credits on each transaction, you make sure that the debits always equal the credits, a key goal of bookkeeping. If the debits do not equal the credits at the end of the period, (month, quarter or year), it indicates that a mistake was made somewhere and one of the transactions was entered improperly. By using this system, the Accounting Equation always stays in balance after each transaction is recorded, in that you are increasing or decreasing both sides of the equation by equal amounts. There is a standard way of dealing with debits and credits assigned to assets, liabilities, owner's equity, revenues, and expenses. Figure 7.2 below summaries this concept:

Figure 7.2

Transaction	Journal Entry
Assets Increase	Debit
Assets Decrease	Credit
Liabilities Increase	Credit
Liabilities Decrease	Debit
Revenue (OE Increases)	Credit
Expense (OE Decreases)	Debit

Now let's record in the general journal some of the transactions of the previous chapters. It is important to remember that every single transaction in the journal must be recorded as both a debit and a credit. First, Dr. Sarah invested $120,000 in her company. This transaction would be recorded as shown in Figure 7.3:

Figure 7.3

JOURNAL

			Amounts	
Date	Entries	Reference	Debits	Credits
2011 Jan 1	Cash		$120,000	
	Owner's Investment			$120,000

You already know that whenever the owner of a business invests cash into his/her business, cash is increased and so is the owner's investment (part of Owner's Equity). If cash (an asset) increases, this is shown as a debit in the journal; the increase in owner's equity is listed as a credit. (See Figure 7.2 above).

In the next transaction, the company buys Equipment and Furniture for $100,000, Computers and Computer Software for $45,000 each. Since the Dr. Sarah does not have sufficient cash to pay for these assets and further assets as well as have sufficient working capital (cash), the company decides to borrow $200,000. This transaction would be recorded in the general journal as shown in Figure 7.4:

Figure 7.4

JOURNAL

			Amounts	
Date	Entries	Reference	Debits	Credits
2011 Jan 3	Cash		$10,000	
	Equipment and Furniture		$100,000	
	Computers		$45,000	
	Computer Software		$45,000	
	Bank Loan Payable			$200,000

Notice in the above journal entry, DEBITS were used to increase the assets (Cash, Equipment and Furniture, Computers and Computer Software), while CREDITS was used to increase the liability Bank Loan Payable. Thus, depending upon which side of the accounting equation the account appears, this will determine if it is recorded as a debit or a credit (See Figure 7.2).

Now we'll move on to the transactions from Chapter 4 which were recorded on the Income Statement.

During the year, the Medical Care Company had income of $129,000. Assuming that cash was collected for all of the services that Dr. Sarah provided, these services would increase cash and would also increase Retained Earnings (through Income).

These transactions would be recorded in the general journal as seen below in Figure 7.5:

Figure 7.5

JOURNAL

Date	Entries	Reference	Debits	Credits
			Amounts	
2011	Cash		$129,000	
5 Jan				
	Income			$129,000

Referring back to the Accounting Equation, $A = L + OE$, the sales transaction has increased the left side (the asset Cash) by $129,000, and increased the right side, Owner's Equity by the same amount.

Looking at another transaction in Chapter 4, Operating Expenses, you can see the impact on the general journal. On January 7, Desert Medical Care Company pays the employees their first week's pay of, assuming, $1000. This transaction would be recorded in the general journal as shown below in Figure 7.6:

Figure 7.6

JOURNAL

			Amounts	
Date	**Entries**	**Reference**	**Debits**	**Credits**
2011	Cash		$1,000	
7 Jan	Salary Expense			$1,000

This transaction has decreased the left side of the accounting equation, Assets or Cash by $1000, and has also decreased the right side owner's equity with an expense by the same amount. Once again, the debits equal the credits.

Finally look at one more transaction from Chapter 4, where Desert Health Care Company incurs interest on the $200,000 bank loan. At the end of January, the company must pay one month's interest expense. Total interest on the loan is $12,000 per year (6% of $200,000). Thus, for one month, the interest expense is $1,000 ($12,000/ 12 months). -This transaction is recorded in the general journal as follows in Figure 7.7:

Figure 7.7

JOURNAL

Date	Entries	Reference	Amounts	
			Debits	Credits
2011	Cash		$1,000	
31 Jan	Interest Expense			$1,000

Once again, notice that Interest Expense is increased by $1,000, which reduces net income and thus, reduces Retained Earnings. Cash, an asset, is decreased by the same amount, and thus the accounting equation stays in balance by reducing assets (left side) and Retained Earnings (or Equity) by the same amount.

The General Ledger

During the month, the journal entries made to record the January transactions would be posted from the general journal to the general ledger. The general ledger is a book containing a record of each account. Posting is simply the process of transferring the information from the general journal to the individual account pages in the general ledger. The cash account, which probably is the first page (or pages) in the general ledger, would look like the example in Figure 7.8:

Figure 7.8

LEDGER

Cash					Account #101			
Date	Comments	Ref	Debit Amount		Date	Comments	Ref	Credit Amount

Notice that the account has two sides. As before, the left side is used to record the debits and the right side is used to record the credits.

Notice that the sample ledger account in Figure 7.8 lists an account number, 101 in the upper right hand corner. Every asset, liability, owner's equity, revenue and expense item has a number assigned to it. Usually, the assets are the 100's, the liabilities the 200's, the owner's equity the 300's, the revenues the 400's, and the expenses the 500's. In the ledger, each item (or account) has a separate page with a separate number. In this case, cash has been assigned the number 101, and all cash transactions are recorded on this page.

The accounts are usually numbered for a variety of reasons. For example, to facilitate referencing or for use instead of the account name. This listing of accounts is normally called the chart of accounts.

After posting the first journal entry (January 1), the cash account would look like Figure 7.9:

Figure 7.9

LEDGER

Cash					Account #101			
Date	Comments	Ref	Debit Amount		Date	Comments	Ref	Credit Amount
Jan 1		J-1	$120,000					

The date of the transaction is entered in the date column on the left-hand side since the entry was a debit. J-1 is entered in the reference column and that tells you that the journal entry that recorded the transaction can be found on page one of the general journal. $120,000 is entered in the left-hand amount column.

The other half of this first journal entry (the credit) would be posted to the Owner's Investment account and would be recorded as shown in Figure 7.10:

Figure 7.10

LEDGER

	Cash					Account #01		
Date	Comments	Ref	Debit Amount		Date	Comments	Ref	Credit Amount
					Jan 1		J-1	$120,000

Of course, in this instance the data is posted to the right-hand column since the entry is a credit to the account.

Now after posting the first entry, the general journal would appear as shown in Figure 7.11:

Figure 7.11

To record $120,000 investment by owner

JOURNAL

Date	Entries	Reference	Amounts	
			Debits	Credits
2011	Cash	101	$120,000	
Jan 1	Owner's Equity	301		$120,000

You see that the account numbers for the cash and owner's investment accounts have now been entered in the reference column of the journal. This step completes the posting process for the first journal entry. The same procedure is repeated until all the journal entries have been posted to the general ledger.

Trial Balance

Typically, accountants and bookkeepers will prepare a trial balance from the general ledger after all transactions have been recorded and posted. A trial balance is merely a list of all accounts in the general ledger that have a balance other than zero, with the balance in each account shown and the debits and credits totaled. A trial balance of Desert Medical Care Company at January 31, 2011 would look like the one in Figure 7.13:

Figure 7.13

DESERT MEDICAL CARE COMPANY
Trial Balance
January 31, 2011

(Before Adjusting & Closing Entries)

Cash...$95,500
Supplies..30,000
Computers...45,000
Computer Software......................................45,000
Equipment & Furniture..............................100,000

Bank Loan Payable (Long-Term)..............................200,000
Owner's Investment..120,000
Retained Earnings...-0-
Income..9,000
Salary Expense..........................10,000
Rent & Utility Expense................2,000
Office Expense.........................1,500
Totals...................................$329,000

$329,000

First turning through the pages of the general ledger and locating each account with a balance other than zero, a list is made of all of these balances. This list is called the trial balance.

Generally speaking, the trial balance is prepared for two reasons. The first reason is to determine whether the total debits equal the total credits. If they do not equal, some kind of error has been made either in the recording of the journal entries or in the posting of the general ledger. In either case the error must be located and corrected. The second reason is to facilitate the preparation of adjusting entries (discussed in the next section) that are necessary before the financial statements can be prepared.

You should note that if Desert Medical Care Company had been in operation prior to this year, a retained earnings figure would appear on the present trial balance. The retained earnings account will show the beginning retained earnings until the accountant closes the accounts that affect the retained earnings by the amount of the profit or loss for the period (month, quarter or year). For more information on closing accounts, see Closing Journal Entries below.

Adjusting Journal Entries

Accounting records are not kept up to date at all times. To do so would be a waste of time, effort, and money because much of the information is not needed for day-to-day decisions. Adjusting entries is a step taken to recognize financial events that have occurred prior to the financial statements' issuance date but which have not been recorded in the journal. These are not transactions with a particular date attached, but they are financial realities that require documentation in order to maintain accurate records. In the case of the Desert Medical Care Company there are several items that need to be adjusted at the end of each month: Accumulated Depreciation on the Computers, Computer Software and Equipment and Furniture. Also each year the company needs to determine the amount of interest on the bank loan. After the adjusting journal entries are recorded in the journal, they must be posted to the accounts in the general ledger, just like the earlier journal entries.

Depreciation Expense

All Long-term assets, except for Land, have a finite life. Their original (historical) cost is therefore spread over their useful lives. This process is called depreciation. In order to depreciate these assets, you need to know what the life expectancy of each is, that is how long these assets will produce income for the business. In our example, you can assume that the Equipment and Furniture has a life expectancy of 10 years, and the computers and computer software of 5 years. To depreciate these two assets, you can divide the historical cost by the life expectancy.

Equipment and Furniture:

$100,000 (historical cost) / 5 years (life expectancy) = $20,000 Depreciation per year

Computers and Computer Software:

$90,000 (historical cost) / 10 years (life expectancy) = $9,000 Depreciation per year

Since you are only looking for the depreciation adjustment for these assets for the month of January, each number would be divided by 12 (months) to arrive at depreciation adjustment for the month of January.

Furniture and Equipment = $20,000 (depreciation per year) / 12 (months per year) = $1,666.67 per month

Computers and Computer Software = $9,000 (depreciation per year) /12 (months per year) =$750.00 per month

☞ Quick Tip:

The Life Expectancy of an Asset: One of the assumptions you as the owner of a business need to make is what the life expectancies of long term assets are. How should you do this? The easiest way is to estimate based on your experience of similar assets used in the business in the past. You can also get information from the library on what averages are used for similar assets in your industry. Finally, the IRS has a schedule of long-term assets, with life expectancy figures they will accept. The final decision is yours, and if reasonable, it is acceptable.

Interest Expense

As you remember, Desert Medical Care Company has to pay interest on the Bank Loan that it took out to buy some of the assets. The loan was $200,000 for 10 years at 6% per year. The total interest per year is $12,000 ($200,000 x 6%). Therefore, each month the business owes the bank one-twelfth of the year's total interest or $1,000 ($12,000/12 months). Since the cash is not owed until the end of the year, Desert Medical Care Company has created another liability called Interest Payable that is due at the end of the year. The amount of this liability is the same as the Interest Expense of $1,000 for the month of January.

QUIZ

How would you "journalize" the following transactions?

- (January 1) Laurel and Hardey invest $100,000 into their new book publishing business.
- (January 3) The two then buy a delivery truck for $20,000. He gives the car dealership $15,000 and takes out a 2-year loan at 6% interest per year for the balance.
- (January 3) Laurel and Hardey then rent space in a warehouse to do his printing. The monthly rent for January is $1200 per month and is due at the beginning of the month (from the 1st to the 3rd). The two pay for this in cash.
- (January 10) Laurel and Hardey then buy a printing press for $6,000 (cash of $4000, and a long-term 8% loan for $2,000) and supplies for $3,000 (cash of $1,000 and a short-term loan of $2,000) Hint: These are two separate entries.
- (January 15) And finally, Laurel and Hardey pay their two employees their first half of the month salary of $3,000 (for the two of them) they pay in cash and the other half they will pay in two days.

The answers appear at the end of this chapter.

Trial Balance after Adjustments

After the adjusting entries are posted to the journal, the accountant may prepare another trial balance to help in the preparation of the actual financial statements, or the accountant may be able to prepare the statements by using the general ledger only. A trial balance prepared at the end of January, 2011 would look like Figure 7.14:

Figure 7.14

DESERT MEDICAL CARE COMPANY
Trial Balance
(After Adjustments, Before Closing)
January 31, 2011

Cash	$95,500	
Supplies	30,000	
Furniture and Equipment	100,000	
Accumulated Depreciation	(1,666.67)	
Computers	45,000	
Accumulated Depreciation	(375)	
Computer Software	45,000	
Accumulated Depreciation	(375)	
Retirement Payable		1,000
Interest Payable		1,000
Mortgage Payable (Long-Term)		200,000
Owner's Investment		120,000
Retained Earnings		-0-
Income		9,000
Rent and Utility Expense	2,000	
Retirement Expense	1,000	
Office Expense	1,500	
Salaries Expenses	10,000	
Depreciation Expense	2,416.67	
Interest Expense	1,000	
	$331,000	$331,000

There are some differences between this trial balance and the one in Exhibit 7.13, which shows the trial balance before the adjusting journal entries. First, some new accounts have been created: Accumulated Depreciation—Computers, Accumulated Depreciation—Computer Software, Accumulated Depreciation—Furniture and Equipment, Depreciation Expense, Retirement Expense and Retirement Payable, Interest Expense and Interest Payable.

The Depreciation Expense account was created to represent the depreciation on the three long-term assets, Furniture and Equipment, Computers and Computer Software. Instead of reducing the long-term assets directly as these long-term assets get older, accountants set up another separate contra-asset account. For long-term assets the contra account is called Accumulated Depreciation. Each long-term asset has a separate contra-asset account. (e.g. Accumulated Depreciation-Furniture and Equipment). On the Balance Sheet, the contra-assets would appear like those shown in Figure 7.15 below:

Figure 7.15

Partial Balance Sheet

Current Assets:

Cash..$95,500
Supplies...30,000

Long-Term Assets:

Furniture and Equipment...$100,000
Less: Accumulated Depreciation..(1,666.67)
Compute..$45,000
Less: Accumulated Depreciation..(375)
Computer
Software...$45,000
Less: Accumulated Depreciation..(375)

Land, even though it is a long-term asset, does not depreciate, and does not have an accumulated depreciation contra-asset account.

Another two accounts we see on the Adjusted Trial Balance are Retirement Expense and Retirement Payable. These two accounts were created because each year the company has to set aside money for the retirement plan of the employees. Since this amount is not funded (that is put into a bank account) until the end of the year, each month when financial statements are prepared, the company has to indicate that it owes this money to the bank account to be used upon retirement by the employees. This is done by debiting a new account called Retirement expense, and crediting a new liability account called Retirement Payable. At the end of the year when the amount is funded, cash will be reduced and so will the liability account.

The last new account is Interest Expense and Interest Payable. These accounts represent the amount of interest that will be paid. In our example, this is $1000 per month on the Bank Loan. Thus, until the Interest is paid, a liability is set up to represent the fact that the company has incurred an expense (time has passed so interest is due on the loan) but has not been paid, thus, the Interest Payable account.

Closing Journal Entries

In general, accounting records are closed at the end of the year. After the closing journal entries have been made and posted, all the income statement accounts (also called temporary accounts) begin the new year with a zero balance. For example, next year we want to accumulate and show in the income account the total income made during that year and that year only; to do this, the income account must have a zero balance at the beginning of the year, so the figures from the previous year don't carry over.

When Desert Medical Care Company decides to make the financial statements for the end of the month, the accountant would make the following entries in the general journal as shown in Figure 7.16 to close the records for January, 2011:

Figure 7.16

To record $120,000 investment by owner

JOURNAL

Date	Entries	Reference	Amount Debits	Amount Credits
2011 31 Jan	Income		$9,000	
			$1,000	
		Salary Exp.		$10,000
		Rent and Util. Exp.		$2,000
		Office Exp.		$1,500
		Retirement Exp.		$1,000
		Depreciation Exp.		$2416.67
		Interest Exp.		$1,000
		Retained Earnings	$8916.67	

Each revenue and expense account is closed (brought to a zero balance) by (1) determining the balance of the account and (2) placing this amount (the account balance) on the opposite side of the account, that is, a debit balance for an account is balanced out on the credit side of the journal and a credit balance is balanced out on the debit side. For example, prior to closing, the Income account had a credit balance of $10,000. To close the Income account it was debited for $9,000, to achieve the desired zero balance. The Rent and Utility Expense account had a debit balance of $2,000, thus, to close this account it was credited for $2,000.

After all of the revenues and expenses have been closed (made to have a zero balance), and the debits and credits are added in the journal, there will be a dollar difference. In the example this difference is the difference between the Income debit and the credits for the various expenses of $8,916.67. This represents net loss for the month of January. (It is a net loss because the expenses are greater than the income). In order to make the closing entry balance an additional debit is needed; this credit is to Retained Earnings. As you learned in previous lessons, Retained Earnings is the account where profits are accumulated from year to year.

☞ Quick Tip:

Handling Revenue and Expense Accounts: Revenue and Expense accounts are temporary accounts. You can close them any time you want summarized information about their financial position. At the end of the accounting period all Revenue and Expense accounts are closed into the Retained Earnings account. This leaves all of the Revenue and Expense accounts with a zero balance after the closing process, and lets the statement reader know how much profit or loss has been created by the business.

Before posting the closing entries, the Income and Rent and Utility Expense accounts (for example) looked like Figure 7.17:

Figure 7.17

LEDGER

Income — Account #401

Date	Comments	Ref	Debit Amount	Date	Comments	Ref	Credit Amount
2011				2011			
				Jan 6		J-1	$500
				Jan 15		J-2	$4,500
				Jan 21		J-3	$4,000

Rent and Utility Expense — Account #508

Date	Comments	Ref	Credit Amount	Date	Comments	Ref	Credit Amount
2011							
Jan 6		J-1	$200				
Jan 15		J-2	$900				
Jan 21		J-3	$900				

After posting the closing entries, the Income and Rent and Utility accounts would look like Figure 7.18:

Figure 7.18

LEDGER

Income   Account #401

Date	Comments	Ref	Debit Amount	Date	Comments	Ref	Credit Amount
				2011			
2011				Jan 6		J-1	$500
				Jan 15		J-2	$4,500
				Jan 21		J-3	$4,000
				Jan 31	Closing	J-5	$9,000

Rent and Utility Expense   Account #508

Date	Comments	Ref	Credit Amount	Date	Comments	Ref	Credit Amount
2011							
Jan 6		J-1	$200				
Jan 15		J-2	$900				
Jan 21		J-3	$900				
Jan 31	Closing	J-5	$2,000				

The double lines drawn across the accounts are meant to indicate that the accounts are closed. Entries for the following period (in this example, February, 2011) would be posted to these accounts in the spaces under the double lines. All of the accounts that were closed would look like the Income and Rent and Utility accounts illustrated above in that the debits and credits would balance, except, of course, the dates and dollars figures would be different.

Often accountants will prepare an after-closing trial balance to see that the debits and credits are still in balance and to see that all the temporary accounts have been closed. Desert Medical Care Company's after-closing trial balance would look like Figure 7.19. Notice that accumulated depreciation is listed as a subtraction on the debit side.

Figure 7.19

DESERT MEDICAL CARE COMPANY
Trial Balance (After Closing)
January 31, 2011

	Credits	Debits
Cash..	$95,500	
Supplies...	30,000	
Furniture and Equipment........................	100,000	
Accumulated Depreciation-F & E............	(1666.67)	
Computers..	45,000	
Accumulated Depreciation-Computers......	(375)	
Computer Software..................................	45,000	
Accumulated Depreciation-Software..........	(375)	
Retirement Payable.................................		1,000
Interest Payable......................................		1,000
Bank Loan Payable (Long-Term)..............		200,000
Owner's Investment.................................		120,000
Retained Earnings...................................		(8,916.67)
Totals..	$313,083.33	

The closing process is a fairly routine one. It merely reverses the balances in the income statement accounts, bringing the ending balances to zero. Thus, since income has a credit balance at the end of the accounting period, to close this account you must debit it to bring its balance to zero. Just the opposite happens with expenses; that is, they normally have a debit balance and to close them they are credited for the same amount. Once all these debits and credits from the closed accounts are totaled on the trial balance, the difference normally would be a credit that is applied to Retained Earnings. This credit balance represents Net Income. In our case, the debits are greater than the credits from the closed accounts. This amount will represent a Net Loss.

In this Chapter you have learned how to record business transactions into the original book of entry—the general journal. You have also learned how to post to the accounting ledgers and how to make adjusting entries. Finally, you have learned how to close the accounting records of a company. In the Corporations chapter, you will learn how the accounting for corporations differs from that of an individual proprietorship.

ANSWERS TO QUIZ

- January 1
  - ➢ Dr: Cash $100,000
  - ➢ Cr: Investment $100,000
  - ➢ Laurel and Hardey invests $100,000 in cash)
- January 3
  - ➢ Dr: Truck (Long-Term Asset) $20,000
  - ➢ Cr: Cash $15,000

- ➢ Cr: Notes Payable (Long-Term Liability) $5,000
- ➢ (To purchase a Truck with cash and credit)
- January 3
  - ➢ Dr: Rental Expense $1,200
  - ➢ Cr: Cash $1,200
  - ➢ (To pay January Rent)
- January 10
  - ➢ Dr: Printing Press (Long-term Asset) $6,000
  - ➢ Cr: Cash $4,000
  - ➢ Cr: Notes Payable $2,000
  - ➢ (To purchase Printing Press with Cash and Long-Term Debt)
- January 10
  - ➢ Dr: Supplies Expense $3,000
  - ➢ Cr: Cash $1,000
  - ➢ Cr: Accountants Payable (Short-Term Debt) $2,000
  - ➢ (To buy supplies for the month with cash and on credit)
- January 15
  - ➢ Dr: Salaries Expense $3,000
  - ➢ Cr: Cash $1,500
  - ➢ Cr: Salaries Payable $1,500
  - ➢ (To pay salaries for the first half of January)

Glossary

Adjusting Journal Entries: Journal entries made at the end of the accounting period (month, quarter and/or year) to recognize transactions that have occurred prior to the statements' issue date, but which have not yet been recorded in the journal. Examples of these entries include: depreciation; salaries earned, but not yet paid; adjustments to prepaid items, like insurance and interest on the mortgage which has not yet been paid.

Chart of Accounts: A listing of account numbers for each of the accounts. These numbers are usually divided into five groups; 100s for assets, 200s for liabilities, 300s for owner's equity, 400s for revenues and 500s for expenses. Every time any accounting entry is made, the accountant will use the same account number for that particular asset, liability, owner's equity, revenue, or expense.

Closing Journal Entries: The process required to bring all accounts to a zero balance. This process is done at the end of the period (month, quarter, or year) prior to the preparation of the financial statements. Only revenues and expenses (also called temporary accounts) are closed, and the difference between revenues and expenses if recorded as net income or net loss.

Credit: The right side of the amount column in a journal or ledger. Credits are recorded when assets and expenses are reduced and when liabilities, owner's equity and revenue accounts are increased.

Debit: The left side of the amount column in a journal or ledger. Debits are recorded when assets and expenses are increased, and when liabilities, owner's equity and revenue accounts are decreased.

Depreciation: The process of spreading the historical cost of a long-term asset over its useful life. In order to determine this amount, management must make an assumption as to the life of all of the long-term assets. The historical cost is then spread evenly over this life expectancy. When this method of depreciation is used (evenly spread over the life) it is called the straight-line method of depreciation.

General Journal: The book in which transactions are first recorded, often referred to as "the book of original entry." As soon as a business transaction takes place, it is recorded in the general journal. The accounts impacted by the transaction, the date, the debits, credits and an explanation of the transaction are also recorded.

General Ledger: A book containing a page (or pages) for every account in the business. After a transaction is recorded in the general journal, the components are then transferred (or posted) to the individual accounts in the general ledger. Thus at any one time, one can review the individual accounts in the general ledger to determine their current balances.

Journal Entries: As soon as a business transaction occurs an entry is made in the general journal to recognize this transaction. A debit (or debits) and a credit (or credits) will be made to the accounts that are impacted by this transaction. The debits and credits for each transaction will always be equal.

Posting: The process of transferring the information in the general journal to the individual accounts in the general ledger. At any time, one can review the individual accounts in the general ledger to determine their balances.

Trial Balance: A list of all accounts in the general ledger that have a balance other than zero. This is prepared right before the financial statements to make sure that the accounts are in balance and that all journal entries have been prepared correctly and accurately. If the trial balance does not balance (that is, debits do not equal credits), it indicates that there has been an error made in either the recording of the transactions in the general journal or in the posting of those transactions to the general ledger. (This does not include a trial balance which has been completed after the closing of accounts).

Chapter 8

Using Financial Statements for Short-Term Analysis

This chapter covers the following information:

✓ **Using Short-Term ratios**

✓ **Current and Quick ratios**

✓ **Working Capital**

✓ **Composition of Assets**

Using Short-Term Ratios

Financial statements can be extremely useful for evaluating a company's future in the near-term (usually defined as one to twelve months) as well as beyond the short-term. This chapter will focus on near term evaluation; evaluation beyond the near-term will be the focus of chapter 9.

The most important question to be answered when evaluating a company's near-term future is whether or not the company will be able to pay its debts when they come due. If the company cannot, it may be forced into bankruptcy or perhaps even forced to cease operations. As you learned earlier, even a profitable company can become short on cash and place its future in jeopardy.

Certain financial statement users will be particularly interested in the short-term prospects of a company. For example, bankers who have made or are contemplating making short-term loans (thirty-day, sixty-day, or even six-month loans) are mainly concerned with determining whether the borrowing company will be able to repay their loans when they come due. These statement users will attempt to forecast the company's cash flow for the period of time during which their loans are expected to be outstanding. For this reason the Statement of Cash Flows discussed in Chapter 5 becomes very important.
Even those users who are mostly interested in the short-term will also have an interest in the long-term. Again, taking banks as an example, bankers must be aware of what is happening now and what the future looks like for all of their customers in order to decide to whom they can loan money and in order to estimate their own future cash flows.

Figure 8.1 gives some examples of how certain financial statement users might use short-term ratios.

Figure 8.1: How Short-Term Ratios are Used

Users	Ratios	Use
Bankers	Current Ratio Working Capital	To make short-term loans
Vendors	Quick Ratio	To extend credit for purchases
Credit Card Co.	Current Ratio Working Capital	To issue credit cards
Business Owners	All	On-going short-term analysis of their business

There are a number of key figures that are useful in these assessments. They are highlighted in figure 8.1 and listed in figure 8.2.

Figure 8.2: Key Short-Term Ratios

Ratio	Calculation
Current Ratio	Current Assets/Current Liabilities
Quick Ratio	Quick Asset/Current Liabilities
	[Quick Assets = Current Assets – Inventory – Prepaid Items]
	Current Assets – Current Liabilities
Working Capital	Accounts Receivable/Average Income per day
Average Collection Period	(Average Income/Day = Annual Income/365)

Current and Quick Ratios

To figure out whether a company is going to survive in the short-term, you should look first at the Balance Sheet. Compare the company's Current Assets with their Current Liabilities (debts that must be paid within twelve months) using the current ratio.

Current Ratio =

Current or Short-Term Assets/Current or Short-Term Liabilities

Also widely used is the comparison of the company's quick Assets—those Current Assets that can be quickly turned into cash—to the Current Liabilities. Usually quick Assets include cash, current receivables, and marketable securities; or in other words, Current Assets minus Inventory and prepaid items. This ratio of quick Assets to Current Liabilities is referred to as the quick (or acid test) ratio.

Quick Asset Ratio = Quick Assets/Current or Short-Term Liabilities

Referring to Figure 3.4 in chapter 3, the current ratio for the Desert Medical Care Company would be 3.87. This is calculated by dividing the Short-Term Assets on December 31, 2011, of $120,000 by the Short-Term Liabilities on the same day of $31,000. Again using the values from figure 3.4, the quick ratio for the medical practice would be 1.91. This is calculated by taking the quick Assets on December 31, 2006, of $59,050 and dividing them by the Current Liabilities of $31,000. But what do these numbers mean?

Before you can decide whether a company has sufficient Current Assets or quick Assets to cover their Current Liabilities, you need to know what the current and quick ratios were in the preceding periods. The rule of thumb is that the current ratio should be greater than 2.0.

What this means is that the Current Assets available to the company to pay their debts are at least double their Current Liabilities. These ratios vary from industry to industry, and therefore the company's current ratio should not only be compared to prior years and to the rule of thumb figure, but should also be compared to similar companies in the medical field.

In general, the larger the current and quick ratios are, the greater the probability that a company will be able to pay its debts in the near term.

In the case of the Desert Medical Care Company, the current and quick ratios are well above the rule of thumb, which means the business is in a very good position to be able to pay its Current Liabilities.

↪Alert

Knowing the environmental conditions that existed in prior periods as compared to now, and having data about similar companies in the same industry are also useful. You can get the average ratios for various industries from publications such as *Moody's, Standard & Poor, Dun & Bradstreet,* or *Robert Morris Associates.*

☞ Quick Tip:

Working Capital

Another important factor to consider in the short-term in addition to these two ratios is the company's working capital. This is calculated by subtracting the Current Liabilities from the Current Assets.

Working Capital = Current or Short-Term Assets – Current or Short-Term Liabilities

Working capital is a cushion. It allows a manager to make errors in an estimate of future cash receipts and disbursements, and still be able to pay its debts when they come due. For example, if a manager estimates both cash receipts and disbursements for the next thirty days to be

$30,000, and for some reason receipts only total $25,000 and disbursements total $35,000, the company must have either sufficient working capital at the beginning of the month to cover the shortfall or good credit with its bankers. If this is not the case, it will find itself unable to settle its debts and possibly be out of business.

➥Alert

It's All Relative: How do we know what is a good enough cushion? The calculation of working capital will not help a great deal unless it is related to the company's cash flow and to prior year's figures. For example calculating a working capital of $20,000 does not mean anything by itself. However, to know that working capital three years ago was $10,000, two years ago was $14,000, and last year was $17,000 indicates a positive trend that gives more meaning to this year's figure of $20,000. Also important is the economy, the budget for future Current Liabilities, and the need to have excess cash in the business.

In addition, it is necessary to compare the working capital to the cash flow of the company, as you calculated in Chapter 5. How much working capital a company should have depends upon its cash flow. It makes sense that a business that receives and/or disburses an average of $7,000,000 per week should have a larger working capital balance than a company that receives and/or disburses $7,000 per week, because the first business' needs for cash are higher.

In the case of our medical care company, the working capital cushion is very good. It is $89,000 (Current Assets of $120,000 minus the Current Liabilities of $31,000).

☞ Quick Tip:

Working Capital Cushion: Is your working capital cushion large enough? What is your cash flow per month? Is it ever negative? What is your cash flow budget for the future? If you had a normal negative flow of cash in the past, and you have projected a negative flow of cash for the next twelve months, you will need a larger working capital cushion than if your projections are the opposite. Also what are your predictions for the economy over the next twelve months? If you expect a slowdown that might affect your industry and company, you will want to have a larger cushion for working capital since you will likely have less Revenue coming in to help you cover your debts.

Composition of Assets

In deciding whether a company is going to survive the near-term, you also want to look at the composition of their Current Assets; that is, you want to see that each of the various Current Asset items is a desirable size. Your main interest here centers on receivables.

Receivables may become too large because patients delay their payments or because the company changed its credit policy so that services are provided to people who are slower in paying off their debts. Once you decide that the company is going to survive in the near future, you can turn to estimating its long-term future prospects. As you begin to look beyond the short-term success of a company, the main focus of your attention shifts from information presented on the Balance Sheet to information presented on the Income Statement in order to look at past performance and project any trends into the future.

The long-term future of a company depends, to a very large extent, upon the effectiveness of the company's employees. One of your main goals is to determine how well the employees have done in the past and how well they are doing now. The information that you have already gathered at the beginning of this chapter with regard to the short-term future prospect gives you valuable clues as to current performance.

However, this is not sufficient to draw a reliable conclusion about the long-term prospects of the company. Chapter 9 will detail how to approach making this sort of evaluation.

Glossary

Current Ratio: A short-term financial analytical tool calculated by dividing Current Assets by Current Liabilities. The rule of thumb is that this ratio should be greater than 2.0; however, this will vary somewhat from company to company. Thus it is necessary to know prior year figures as a basis of comparison.

Quick Ratio (or Acid Test Ratio): A short-term financial analytical tool calculated by dividing Quick Assets by Current Liabilities. The rule of thumb for this ratio is that it should be above 1.5. However, as with the current ratio, the history of the company's ratio should be considered.

Working Capital: A short-term financial analytical tool calculated by subtracting Current Liabilities from Current Assets. To determine what is a safe and comfortable cushion (sufficient to cover whatever debts may come due), this figure needs to be compared to the cash flow of the company as well as to prior years' data.

Chapter 9

Using Financial Statements for Long-Term Analysis

This chapter covers the following information:

✓ Rate of Return on Investment

✓ Revenue-Based Ratios or Percentages

✓ Earnings Data

✓ Long-term Debt Position

✓ Dividend Data

✓ Footnotes

✓ Quality of Earnings

In Chapter 8 we reviewed several ratios that are beneficial in analyzing the short-term viability of a company. In Figure 9.1 below, we see that there are also several ratios that need to be reviewed and evaluated to understand the long-term strength of a company. Each of these ratios will be discussed in this chapter.

Figure 9.1: Long-term Information

Used to Evaluate a Company

1. Rate of return on investment

2. Net profit as a percentage of revenue

3. Percentage of various expenses to revenue

4. Rate of growth of revenue

5. Earnings per share

6. Extraordinary gains and losses

7. Price/earnings ratio

8. Number of times interest and preferred stock dividends were earned

9. Total liabilities to total assets

10. Dividend payout ratio

Rate of Return on Investment

The rate of return on investment is probably the single most important financial statistic. It comes as close as any figure can to reflecting how well a company has done.

Return on Investment (ROI) is usually calculated as follows:

Rate of return (as a ratio) = Net Income/Average Stockholders' or Owner's Equity

Rate of return (as a percentage) = Net Income/ Average Stockholders' or Owner's Equity (x 100)

NOTE: Stockholder's Equity is the term used in a corporation, whereas, Owner's Equity is the term used in a proprietorship and partnership. They are similar in that they both show how much the owner(s) invested in the business plus their accumulated earnings (Retained Earnings).

This ratio depicts how much money was earned as compared to the amount the owners invested in the business. In the example in Chapter 3, Dr. Sarah had invested $120,000 into the business on January 1. Since the beginning Owner's Equity was $0 on January 1, and the ending Owner's Equity was $99,000 on December 31, the average for the year was $49,500.   Since the Net Loss for 2011 was $21,000, Dr. Sarah had a negative return on her investment of 42.4% on her investment ($21,000/$49,500). In the majority of medical practices, a loss is expected in the first couple of years.

What is a good return on the owner's investment? The only way to answer this question is to know what alternative investments an investor might consider. Can the owner invest money elsewhere and make more money? If the answer is NO, then the return is a good one. This analysis should be made on an on-going basis in order to continually determine where to invest one's money.

Having said this, there are exceptions. In the early years of a new company, the owner may not make a great return or any return. But the owner may be "betting" on the future, in the belief that the returns will outpace other alternatives. In addition, a company should consider how well it does in the current year as compared to the previous year by comparing the rate of return figure for each of the two years. Comparing one company's results to those of another company in the same industry is also a useful indicator of how the company is doing in comparison to the competition.

↪Alert

Revenue-Based Ratios or Percentages

In order to be able to predict future profitability, you need to examine your company's and other companies' past revenue and expenses.

One such ratio that aids in the analysis of future profitability is the Net Profit as a Percentage of Revenue.

Net Profit as a Percentage of Revenue = (Net Income / Revenue) x 100

An increase in this percentage as compared to previous years may indicate that the company is operating more efficiently. More revenue was made with fewer expenses. Also, when the net profit as a percentage of revenue is higher for one company than another, it may indicate that one company has been operating more efficiently than the other.

In the case of the Desert Medical Care Company, net loss for 2011 was $21,000. Revenue for the year was $129,000. Thus, the net loss as a percentage of revenue would be -16.3%. Is this good? Bad? Helpful? Since this is the first year of operations for the company, we do not have any prior years for comparison. However, it does tell us that the company is losing over 16% on their revenue. This loss in the first year of operations of a medical practice must be compared to other similar types of businesses.   If we had the data we could compare this to other medical practices and in the future we will be able to compare it to prior years for the Desert Medical Care Company. (Once again, keep in mind that the different companies being compared must have used the same GAAP to arrive at their net income calculations in order for comparisons to be meaningful).

To help verify these hunches and to gain better insight into operational changes, it is also helpful to compare a variety of different expenses to the total revenue figure. By understanding these ratios of various expenses to revenue, one can determine if a larger or a smaller percentage during the year is being spent on these expenses. If a company is going to be competitive and successful, it must control its expenses. These ratios show the areas of the business where the company has been able to control these expenses.   See Figure 9.2 for several examples.

Figure 9.2: Important Revenue Ratios

1. General and administrative expenses / Revenue

2. Depreciation expenses / Revenue

3. Lease and rental expenses / Revenue

4. Repairs and maintenance expense / Revenue

5. Advertising / Revenue

6. Research and development / Revenue

Another revenue based ratio that is helpful is the rate of growth of revenue from one period to the next, calculated by comparing the increase (or decrease) in revenue between two periods to the revenue in the first period. You would find it very informative to learn that Desert Medical Care Company revenue increased 10% from one year to the next, and 20% from year two to three, and 30% from year three to four, etc. The pattern of revenue over the most recent years of company's life can help you form an estimate of expected future revenue.

Earnings Data

The earnings per share figure (EPS) and the price/earnings ratio (P/E) are, along with the rate of return on investment ratio, the most widely used information about corporations. The price/earnings ratio is calculated by dividing the market price per share of that company's stock by the earnings per share of the company.

Long-Term Debt Position

Some people believe that a company that borrows money is not as good or as well managed as a company that operates without borrowing. This is not necessarily true. Often, by borrowing money, a company can increase the net income for the owners.

For example, say that Company A's assets total $100,000, liabilities total $10,000, and stockholder's equity totals $90,000, expects a net income next year of $9,000. This represents a return on investment of 10%.

Now assume that management is considering the purchase of $40,000 worth of assets. These assets will produce additional annual net income (before interest expense) of $4,000. The company has two choices. First it can borrow the $40,000 at 6% interest or it can have the investors put the additional $40,000 into the business.

In scenario 1, Company A borrows the needed $40,000. Company A's net income next year would be $10,600 ($9,000 + $4,000 - $2,400) before income taxes. The $2,400 reduction to Net Income is the interest on the loan ($40,000 x 6%). Thus, the return on investment would be 11.7% ($10,600 / $90,000 = 11.7%).

In scenario 2, instead of borrowing the $40,000, the owners invest their own money. Net income would still increase by $4,000 to $13,000 ($9,000 + $4,000). There would be no interest expense, and the Return on Stockholder's Equity would be $13,000 / $130,000 the original $90,000 + the additional $40,000). Thus, it's Return on Investment remains at 10%.

Thus, scenario 1, where Company A borrowed the additional $40,000, and ended up with a return on investment of 11.7% was a more favorable outcome.

↪ Alert

Dangerous Debt: Too much debt can make a company too "risky". During economic downturns, these companies may not be able to repay their debts. However, on the other hand, little or no debt may not be a good thing either. If a company can borrow money at 7% interest and earn 10% on their investment, borrowing will increase their overall rate of return.

One way to help you determine if a company has put themselves into a risky position is to calculate two ratios: the number of times interest was earned, and the ratio of total liabilities to total assets.

To calculate the number of times that interest was earned, divide the interest expense into the net income before interest expense and before income taxes. You use the income figure before income taxes because interest expense is deductible for income tax purposes.

Number of Times Interest Was Earned = Net Income Before Interest and Taxes / Interest Expense

The larger this ratio, the easier it is for the company to meet its interest payments, and the less likely it is that the company will default on its loans.

To calculate the ratio of liabilities to assets, you divide total liabilities by total assets.

Ratio of Liabilities to Assets = Total Liabilities / Total Assets

The idea here is that the larger the ratio, the more risky the company. Of course, a company with a large liability to asset ratio may prosper while a company without any debt at all may fail. The liability to asset ratio as well as any ratio only gives you a part of the total picture, and must be analyzed along with other ratios, and outside information about the company, the industry, and the economy.

Dividend Data

Additional information about a company can be obtained by looking at the cash dividends that it has paid over the past several years and calculating the dividend payout ratio, the total cash dividends declared during the year divided by the net income for the year.

Dividend Payout Ratio = Dividends Declared/ Net Income

If the ratio is large, the company is paying out to the stockholders a large portion of the funds earned and not reinvesting them in the company. If this ratio is small or if the company pays no dividends whatsoever, the company may be growing rapidly and using the funds to finance this growth. Which is better? This is completely determined by your personal investment needs if you are a stockholder or the goals of the business if you are part of management.

Figure 9.3 illustrates examples of which long-term ratios are useful for various users.

Figure 9.3: How Long-Term Ratios are Used

Users	Ratios	Used For
Lenders	Number of Times Interest Was Earned	Making Long-Term Loans
Stockholders	Total Liabilities/Total Assets EPS P/E Ratio Dividend Payout Ratio	Purchasing/ Holding Stock
Owners/Managers	Revenue-Based	On-going Long-Term Analysis

Footnotes

Almost all financial statements of companies larger than average small business have footnotes attached to them. The footnotes are as important as the fine print in a contract. When you examine a company's annual report, consider reading the footnotes first. Examine the financial statements next and read the president's message and the rest of the "advertising" last.

Information contained in the footnotes is quite varied. It can include terms of pension plans, terms of stock options outstanding, the nature and expected outcome of any pending lawsuits, terms of a long-term lease agreement, and probable effects of forced sale of properties in a foreign country. You may find an abundance of clues about a company's future from the footnotes.

Analyzing financial statements can be extremely helpful, but without the use of historical data, no predictions could be made about the future of a company. The more you read financial statements, use them and work with them, the better your decisions about the future of your company and those you wish to invest in will become.

In this Chapter you have learned how financial statements and various ratios can be used to evaluate the long-term success of a business In Chapter 10 you will learn how to prepare and use a budget.

Glossary

Dividend Payout Ratio: A long-term financial analytical tool calculated by dividing Dividends Declared by Net Income. This ratio is useful when analyzing how much of the earnings for the year have been distributed to the stockholders. As with all other ratios, it must be compared to prior years and to other companies.

Earnings Per Share: A long-term financial analytical tool calculated by dividing Net income by the average number of common shares outstanding for the year. This ratio can only be calculated for corporations. Sometimes this ratio gets too much attention, when potential investors are making their decisions. This number is only as accurate and useful as is net income itself and must be used in conjunction with many of the other ratios in this chapter.

Extraordinary Gains and Losses: Gains and losses from the sale of items that are neither considered to be recurring nor a normal part of the business operations. For this reason, it is required by GAAP, that these gains and losses be separated on the income statement from income from operations.

Net Profit or Loss as a Percentage of Revenue: A long-term financial analytical tool calculated by dividing net income by revenue and multiplying the results by 100. This ratio should be compared with prior year's figures as well as with industry averages to determine its value to management.

Number of Times Interest Was Earned: A long-term financial analytical tool calculated by dividing net Income before Taxes by

Interest Expense. The larger this number, the more satisfied are the lenders since they will have a higher coverage of the interest due to them by the net income of the company.

Price/Earnings Ratio: A long-term financial analytical tool calculated by dividing market price per share by earnings per share. This ratio can only be calculated for corporations since partnerships and proprietorships do not have stock and thus have no market price or earnings per share.- In general for corporations, the higher this ratio the better and a positive upward trend in this ratio from year to year is looked on favorably by investors.

Rate of Revenue Growth: A long-term financial analytical tool, the percentage change in revenue between two or more years. Generally, businesses look for this figure to grow from year to year.

Rate of Return on Investment: A long-term financial analytical tool calculated by dividing net income by the average stockholders' equity. The average stockholders' equity is determined by adding the beginning of the year equity with the end of the year's and dividing by two. A good rate of return is one that would be greater than what could be earned investing that money in other places, like with the bank or in bonds or securities.

Chapter 10

Budgeting for Your Business and Personal Use

This chapter covers the following information:

✓ What Is a Budget?

✓ Planning and Control

✓ Advantages of Budgeting

✓ Income Budget

✓ Operating Expenses

✓ Budgeted Income Statement

✓ The Cash Budget

What Is a Budget?

The budget is a detailed plan that outlines future expectations in quantitative terms. Budgets in accounting can be used for a variety of reasons. You can use a budget to plan and control your future income and expenses, which would look like the income statements we have been reviewing throughout the book. Or you can use budgets to plan for future capital expenditures, which would show when the company plans to buy long-term assets, and where this money is to come from and when.

Planning and Control

So why would Dr. Sarah want to do a budget for her business? The answer to this question is that Dr. Sarah is going to produce a budget each year for the purpose of **planning** for her company into the future and to **control** the amount she is spending.

The terms planning and control are often used interchangeably in an accounting sense, but they are actually two distinct concepts. Planning is the development of future objectives and the preparation of budgets to meet these objectives. Control on the other hand involves ensuring that the objectives established during the planning phase are attained. A good budgeting system takes into consideration both the plan and the control.

Advantages of Budgeting

Whether the budget is for personal use or for your business, the major advantage of using a budget is that it gives formality to the planning process. If the budget involves other people, it also serves as a way of communicating the plan to these other people. Once the budget has been established it serves as a benchmark for evaluating the actual results.

Without preparing a budget, Dr. Sarah would not know how much money her company is going to have at the end of the month, how much she must borrow to buy the capital assets needed for the business, nor will she know if the revenues are going to exceed the expenses or vice versa. The process of preparing the budget will be critical to Dr. Sarah as she plans for the future. Most small businesses that go out of business do so, not because they don't have a good product or service, but because they have not planned well and run out of cash. Preparing a budget can help avoid this undesirable end.

☞ Quick Tip:

Using Budgets in Your Business: With the use of personal computers and spreadsheet programs, the budgeting process has been simplified. Budgets can be implemented and maintained at little cost. In addition, it is easy to make changes on a regular basis to view potential situations that may come up, thus allowing the individual or the manager to more easily make decisions based on these anticipated results, thus implementing the control feature of a budget.

Income Budget

Let's assume that Dr. Sarah wants to prepare a master budget for the Medical Care Company for the year 2011. In order to prepare this budget, Dr. Sarah is going to have to guesstimate how much revenue the business will generate for the year. As indicated in Figure 10.1, without this first step of creating an income budget, none of the other budgets can be prepared.

Dr. Sarah calculates that the total revenue for 2011 will be $145,000. In addition to the revenue from medical services, the company has been increasing its revenue from sales of associated products, mainly vitamins. During 2011, the revenue from these products will be budgeted at $15,000. The expenses associated with these product sales are budgeted to be $3,600.

Operating Expenses

By looking back at the Master Budget in Figure 10.1 we can see that the income budget flows directly into the budget for operating expenses. As indicated in Figure 4.1, these expenses were $138,000, or 107 percent of revenue for 2011. We would hope that this percentage decreases during the year 2011, let's assume to 85%. Since revenue is budgeted to be $145,000, operating expenses would be budgeted at $123,250 (85% of $145,000).

Capital Budget

The capital budget is concerned with those items that will last longer than one year, that is the company's long-term assets. To determine if any additional space would need to be rented or built, the business must do a long-range sales forecast. Assuming that the business is growing at a fairly constant rate, Dr. Sarah has predicted that within five years a building must be purchased in order to meet the business's demand. Dr. Sarah's research of local real estate indicates that the cost of a building with sufficient space for the next five years would be $148,000. Therefore, the capital budget per month for the next five years (that is, when the purchase will actually have to be made since Dr. Sarah does not want to incur any additional debt by taking out a mortgage on this building) would be $2,466.67 ($148,000/60 months). In order to purchase the building five years from now, $2,466.67 must be set aside every month for the next five years.

With the information that has been gathered to this point, it is now possible to create a cash budget and a budgeted income statement, balance sheet, and cash flow. Let's examine this information.

Budgeted Income Statement

Using the figures calculated above, Dr. Sarah can create a budgeted income statement like the one shown in Figure 10.2:

Figure 10.2: Budgeted Income Statement

DESERT MEDICAL CARE COMPANY
Budgeted Income Statement
For the Year Ended December 31, 2011

Revenue:	$145,000	
Operating Expenses		<u>123,250</u>
Net Income from Operations	21,750	
Other Revenue:		
Other Product Revenue	15,000	
Other Expenses		
Product Purchases		<u>3,600</u>
Net Income	<u>33,150</u>	

Why does the Medical Care Company need this income statement? They might use it to show to the bank to get a loan. They might want to show it to potential partners looking for information about the future of the business, and of course, they will also need it for planning how they are going to expand in the future!

The Cash Budget

Next, the company needs to calculate how much cash they are going to have at the end of the year. Dr. Sarah needs to know this figure in order to prepare the budgeted balance sheet, but more importantly to make sure the company has enough cash to pay its bills in the following periods, and keep the cash balance at a "safe level."

In order to calculate the budgeted ending cash balance for 2011 we need to know the beginning cash balance. This figure is the same as the ending cash balance on December 31, 2011 because the business starts the new year with the amount of cash it ended the last year with. This figure is $9,050 (see figure 3.2). A number of assumptions need to be made as well. Sales for 2011 were predicted to be $145,000 plus $15,000 for other product revenue (for a total of $160,000). Some of this revenue will be written off for various reasons (and in the past it has been Dr. Sarah's experience that this will average 15%, the actual cash that will be received during 2011 from these projected revenues will be $136,000).

Now we need to calculate the cash expenditures for 2011. The first expenditure is that of operating expenses. Above we have guesstimated that the operating expenses will be 85% of the company's revenue for the next year. We have also estimated that with $15,000 of other product sales, the cost associated to these products will be $3,600.

The last cash "expenditure" that the Company made during 2011 is the $4,133.33 per month that the business "put aside" for the future purchase of a building. This cash transaction is neither an expenditure nor a reduction in cash. It is simply going from one bank account to another. The only reason for the transaction at all is to make sure that the cash left in the operating cash account is not accidentally spent prior to the purchase of the building.

Let's take a look below at Figure 10.3 to see how we can actually calculate the ending cash balance.

Figure 10.3: Budgeted Ending Cash Balance

DESERT MEDICAL CARE COMPANY

Budgeted Ending Cash Balance

For the Year Ended December 31, 2011

Beginning Cash	$9,050
Add:	
Cash Receipts from 2011 Revenue	145,000
Cash Receipts from Sale of Other Products	15,000
Subtract:	
Cash Payments for Operating Expenses in 2011	(123,250)
Cash Payments for Other Product Costs in 2011	(3,600)
Ending Cash Balance	$42,200

(Note to the Cash Budget: Of the $42,250 ending cash balance, $29,600 ($2,466.67 x 12 months) has been set aside in a separate bank account for the future purchase of a new building.)

The example presented here is for a small business such as Desert Medical Care Company. However, the same concepts can be applied to preparing a personal budget and the same benefits will be derived.

☞ Quick Tip:

Participation is key: The success or failure of budgets within an organization is usually enhanced by the participation of the managers, who are generally more apt to fulfill the goals that they have had a direct role in developing. This isn't to say that these budgets should not be subject to review by higher management; however, any changes that are made should be done with the involvement of the individuals who played a part in creating the budget.

In this Chapter you learned the meaning of a budget, the value of preparing one, and the ways in which the components interrelate.

Glossary

Budget: A detailed plan which outlines future expectations in quantitative terms. The major purposes of a budget are to plan for the future and to control the operations of the company. The budget is prepared on an on-going basis and adjusted continually with the acquisition of additional information.

Capital Budget: The budget for long-term assets. Not only does this budget help determine what future capital (long-term) assets are needed for the business, but also how much money needs to be set aside each month or quarter to acquire these assets in the future.

Control: Involves ensuring that the objectives established during the planning phase of the budget preparation are attained. For example, once it is determined that the amount of cash needed at the end of the year is $40,000, all during the year, the cash account needs to be monitored by careful review of the budget and decisions made to ensure the desired ending balance is attained.

Master Budget: A network of many separate budgets that are interdependent. The master budget starts with the Sales Budget. Once it is estimated how much in sales is going to occur during the year, all of the other budgets, for inventory, purchases, cash, and expenses, et al, can be determined.

Planning: The development of future objectives and the preparation of budgets to meet those objectives. Without a budget, there is no planning, and companies that attempt to operate their businesses without this type of planning base their success on luck.

Chapter 11

Services Your CPA Can Provide for Your Business

This chapter covers the following information:

✓ What Your CPA Can do For You

✓ What is an Audit

✓ Accounting vs. Auditing

✓ Types of Auditors

✓ The Certified Public Accountant (CPA)

✓ Internal Auditors

✓ Governmental Auditors

✓ Other Types of Reports You might Need

✓ Other Services Provided by Accountants

What Your CPA Can do For You

You probably think of yourself as a medical professional, ONLY. And yes, you are this, but you are also a small business owner. You are running a small business and have all of the same issues and challenges that any other small business owner has. But you don't have a lot of time, you say, to be burdened with the day to day operations of this business. So you hire an office manager, or a bookkeeper or both to take care of these, but still don't understand the reports that they issue to you. That is why you have bought this book and why you are trying to get more involved in understanding your business and not leave everything up to one or two people who have the ability to control or misuse your assets (which is the topic of the next chapter).

Your CPA can help you in several aspects of your business, they can provide financial planning advice, tax advice and preparation, and they can provide financial reports (by doing a compilation) or a review of your financial statements or even an audit (not very usual in a small business). Let's examine what some of these financial services entail.

What Is an Audit?

One of the rules that the Securities Exchange Commission (SEC) has issued is that the financial statements of public companies (those companies selling stock to the public) must be examined by an independent public accountant through the process of an auditor. This rule means that an accountant, who is not an employee of the company and who is licensed to practice as a public accountant by the state where the financial statements are being prepared, must audit (or examine) the records of the company and must determine whether or not the financial statements are in accordance with the rules of Generally Accepted Accounting Principles (GAAP). In addition, the auditor has the responsibility to give reasonable assurance that the financial statements are free of any material misstatement.

When auditors issue accounting reports they must follow a set of rules known as Generally Accepted Auditing Standards (GAAS). These standards have been the jurisdiction of the American Institute of Certified Public Accountants and their Auditing Standards Board. With the passage of the Sarbanes-Oxley Act of 2002, Congress has now taken the responsibility for creating standards for public companies and created the Public Company Accounting Oversight Board (PCAOB) for this purpose. The Board has the additional responsibility to make sure that audit quality is not compromised and that auditor performance meets public expectations.

In addition to the auditing standards, CPAs are expected to follow the Code of Ethics established by the profession. By establishing and adhering to such a code this ensures the auditor's independence—the major attribute the auditor has to sell to the public. (The topic of ethics will be discussed in more depth along with forensic accounting in Chapter 12.)

A typical auditor's report (known as the unqualified report) is issued when the financial statements are in accordance with GAAP. This report is written and issued by the auditors and is submitted to the public with the financial statements.

Remember that the financial statements are prepared by and are the responsibility of the management of the company and not the auditors. Since the major corporate failures of the 1990's and early 2000's, the Sarbanes-Oxley Act of 2002 requires company management to sign a letter stating that the financial statements are presented fairly in accordance with generally accepted accounting principles, just as the auditors must.

Accounting versus Auditing

As discussed in previous chapters, accounting is the process of recording, classifying, and summarizing economic events in a process that leads to the preparation of financial statements.

Auditing, on the other hand, is not concerned with the preparation of the accounting data, but with the evaluation of this data to determine if it is properly presented in accordance with the rules of accounting (GAAP) and whether it properly reflects the events that have occurred during the period in question.

Types of Auditors

An auditor is an individual or company who checks the accuracy and fairness of the accounting records of a company and determines whether the financial statements are in accordance with the Generally Accepted Accounting Principles. There are many different types of auditors. Three of these are listed below.

The Certified Public Accountant (CPA)

Certified Public Accountants (CPAs) are auditors who serve the needs of the general public by providing auditing, tax planning and preparation, and management consulting services. CPAs can work as individuals or as employees of a firm; these firms range in size from one individual to international organizations with thousands of employees.

The largest of these firms have offices worldwide, and are referred to as the "Big Four." Even though they only employ about 12% of all of the CPAs in the United States, they actually perform the audits of about 85% of the largest corporations in the world. These four companies are: Deloitte & Touche, Ernst & Young, KPMG, and PricewaterhouseCoopers.

Those individuals who act as independent auditors must be licensed to perform audits by the state in which they practice. The laws vary from state to state as to the requirements that must be met in order to obtain such licenses. However, to be issued a license to practice as a CPA, all states require the individual to pass a uniform examination, which is prepared and graded by the American Institute of CPAs (AICPA). Prior to taking this examination, an individual must have a minimum of four years of college education, with many states now requiring 5 years. In addition to passing this examination, most states require an individual to have some experience working with another CPA prior to being licensed. Most states also require that after being licensed to practice as a public accountant, CPAs must take at least a certain minimum amount of continuing education coursework each year in order to have their license renewed.

If you ever decide to invest your money into a public company you will be exposed to the audit opinion in the company's annual report. You would normally like to see that the company has received a standard (or clean) audit opinion as shown below in Figure 11.1.

Figure 11.1: The Unqualified Audit Opinion (Standard)

Sydney and Maude
Certified Public Accountants
7 Circle Drive
Cape Cod, MA 02117

Report of Independent Registered Public Accounting Firm

To: the Board of Directors and Shareholders,

The Desert Care Medical Company

We have audited the accompanying balance sheets of The Desert Care Medical Company as of December 31, 2011 and 2010, and the related statements of income, shareholders' equity, and cash flows for the years then ended. These financial statements are the responsibility of the Company's management. Our responsibility is to express an opinion on these financial statements based on our audits.

We conducted our audits in accordance with auditing standards of the Public Company Accounting Oversight Board. Those standards require that we plan and perform the audit to obtain reasonable assurance about whether the financial statements are free of material misstatement. An audit includes examining, on a test basis, evidence supporting the amounts and disclosures in the financial statements. An audit also includes assessing the accounting principles used and significant estimates made by management, as well as evaluating the overall financial statement presentation. We believe that our audits provide a reasonable basis for our opinion.

In our opinion, the financial statements referred to above present fairly, in all material respects, the financial position of The Desert Care Medical Company as of December 31, 2011 and 2010 and the results of its operations and its cash flows for the years then ended in conformity with accounting principles generally accepted in the United States.

Sydney and Maude, CPAs

Cape Cod, Massachusetts

March 17, 2012

➥Alert

Audits Have Their Limits: These audits do not guarantee the dollar accuracy or predictive ability of these financial statements, only that they are presented in accordance with a set of accounting rules (GAAP). Many people believe that the auditor will either stop or detect all fraud within an organization, but this is not necessarily the case. Even though auditors do follow procedures that help detect fraud, they cannot detect or disclose all such instances.

Internal Auditors

Internal auditors are employed by companies to audit the companies' own records. The functions of these auditors vary greatly, depending upon the needs and expectations of management. In general, the work includes compliance audits (to make sure the accounting is in compliance with the rules of the company and the laws under which they operate) and operational audits (a review of an organization's operating procedures for efficiency and effectiveness). Operational Audits review the business for efficient use of resources; they are meant to help management make decisions that will aid the company in becoming more profitable.

As with CPAs, many internal auditors are also certified by passing a nationally prepared examination. This examination is for the Certificate of Internal Auditing and is prepared by the Institute of Internal Auditors.

Governmental Auditors

As you would expect, governmental auditors are individuals who perform the audit function within or on behalf of a governmental organization. As with the other two types of auditors described above, these individuals also must be independent from the individuals or groups that they are auditing.

Examples of governmental organizations that hire and use auditors include: (1) the United States General Accounting Office (GAO). The major function of this group is to perform the audit function for Congress. (2) The Internal Revenue Service which hires auditors to enforce the federal tax laws as defined by the Congress and interpreted by the courts. (3) The Bureau of Alcohol, Tobacco and Firearms (ATF), (4) The Drug Enforcement Agency (DEA), and (5) The Federal Bureau of Investigation (FBI). Rather than following generally accepted accounting principles, government audits are done in accordance with a set of accounting rules established by the Governmental Accounting Standards Board (GASB).

Other Services Provided by Accountants

In addition to audits, CPAs perform many other types of assurance and accounting services. Some of these include historical financial information and other work includes non-historical information.

Examples of the historical information are:

>*Special reports

>*Financial statements prepared for use in other countries

>*Personal financial statements

>*Reviews of interim financial information

>*Compilation of financial statements

In most cases of small business and medical care companies, an audit is not necessary or required. However in order to receive a bank loan, or to admit a new partner, a review may be required. A review is less costly, less in scope, but still gives an independent set of eyes to look at the financial statements and say that they have been "reviewed." An example of a review report by a CPA is shown in Figure 11.3.

Figure 11.3: A Review Report

We have reviewed the balance sheet and related statements of income, retained earnings and cash flows of the Desert Medical Care Company as of September 30, 2011, and for the thee-month and nine-month periods then ended. These financial statements are the responsibility of the company's management.

We conducted our review in accordance with standards established by the American Institute of Certified Public

Accountants. A review of interim financial information consists principally of applying analytical procedures to financial data and making inquires of persons responsible for financial and accounting matters. It is substantially less in scope than an audit conducted in accordance with generally accepted auditing standards, the objective of which is the expression of an opinion regarding the financial statements taken as a whole. Accordingly, we do not express such an opinion.

Based on our review, we are not aware of any material modifications that should be made to the accompanying financial statements for them to be in conformity with generally accepted accounting principles.

Compilations

This is the type of service most used by small business when they do not have the resources to hire a full time bookkeeper or want to keep this process as independent as possible by hiring an outside firm. Compilations involve the preparation of financial statements from accounting records and other information from management. In order to perform a compilation, a CPA must have knowledge of the client's business and industry. At a minimum, the CPA must read the statements for any material errors or major discrepancies from generally accepted accounting principles. If the CPA knows or suspects that the financial statements are going to be relied upon by a third party, they should attach a report, similar to the one in Figure 11.4, to the financial statements.

Figure 11.4: A Compilation Report

We have complied the accompanying balance sheet of the Desert Medical Care Company as of December 31, 2011 and the related statements of income, retained earnings, and cash flows for the year then ended, in accordance with the Statements on Standards for Accounting and Review Services issued by the American Institute of Certified Public Accountants.

A compilation is limited to presenting in the form of financial statements information that is the representation of management. We have not audited or reviewed the accompanying financial statements and, accordingly, do not express an opinion or any other form of assurance on them.

In this Chapter you have learned about different types of auditors/accountants and types of services that they can provide to you in your medical practice.

Glossary

Adverse Audit Report: A type of report issued by a CPA firm at the completion of an audit. This report is issued when the CPA concludes that the financial statements being audited are not in accordance with Generally Accepted Accounting Principles.

Audit: The accumulation and evaluation of evidence about a company's financial statements to determine if they are in accordance with GAAP.

Auditor: The individual who checks the accuracy and fairness of the accounting records of a company and issues a report as to whether the company's financial records are in accordance with Generally Accepted Accounting Principles.

"Big Four" Accounting Firms: The four largest CPA firms in the world with offices worldwide. PricewaterhouseCoopers, KPMG, Deloitt & Touche, and Ernst & Young perform the audits of the majority of the world's large companies.

Certified Public Accountant (CPA): Auditors who serve the needs of the general public. -These individuals have passed an examination, in most cases have 150 hours of college credits, have worked with another CPA for a minimum of two years, and complete a required 20-40 hours of continuing education each year. Their work includes auditing, tax planning and preparation, and management consulting.

Code of Ethics: A set of rules established by the American Institute of Certified Public Accountants to be followed by all CPAs regarding the ethics they should observe in their work as a CPA.

Compilation: Are the preparation of financial statements from accounting records and other information from management. A report may be issued on these statements if the CPA believes that a third-party will rely on the statements.

Compliance Reports: A report that makes sure the accounting is in compliance with the rules being reviewed. Most often these types of reports are governmental in that they determine whether the financial statements are in compliance with government regulations. They can, however, also be used to review compliance in other instances.

Disclaimer Audit Report: A type of report issued by a CPA firm at the completion of an audit. This report is issued when the CPA concludes that he or she does not have enough information to determine whether the financial statements are or are not in accordance with the accounting rules.

Generally Accepted Auditing Standards: A set of standards established by the AICPA and the SEC

Governmental auditors: The individuals who perform the audit function for a governmental organization such as the U.S. General Accounting Office (GAO), the Internal Revenue Service (IRS), the Securities and Exchange Commission (SEC), Bureau of Alcohol, Tobacco and Firearms (ATF), Drug Enforcement Agency (DEA), and the Federal Bureau of Investigation (FBI), as well as state and local governments. Rather than following generally accepted accounting principles, government audits are done in accordance with a set of accounting rules established by the Governmental Accounting Standards Board (GASB).

Governmental Accounting Standards Board: Issues a set of rules to be followed by governmental accountants rather than generally accepted accounting principles.

Internal auditors: These auditors are employed by companies to audit the company's own records. These individuals are not necessarily certified public accountants (CPAs), but many are certified internal auditors (CIA). To ensure autonomy, these individuals report directly to the audit committee or Board of Directors of the company rather than to company management.

Operational Audit: A review of an organization's operating procedures for the purpose of making recommendations about the efficiency and effectiveness of business objectives and compliance with company policy. The goal of this type of an audit is to help managers discharge their responsibilities and maximize profitability.

Public Company Accounting Oversight Board (PCAOB): Established by Congress as part of the Sarbanes-Oxley Law of 2002, the PCAOB is charged with the responsibility of creating accounting standards for public companies. The Board has the additional responsibility to make sure that audit quality is not compromised and that auditor performance meets public expectations.

Qualified Audit Report: A type of report issued by a CPA firm at the completion of an audit. This report is issued when the CPA concludes that the financial statements being audited are presented in accordance with GAAP, except for some specified items being different, for example the use of a non-standard type of inventory valuation is used.

Review: The objective of a review is to provide a basis of communicating whether the CPA is aware of any material modifications or errors with the interim statements.

Sarbanes-Oxley Act (2002): Passed by Congress to include a set of reforms toughening penalties for corporate fraud, restricting types of consulting services for audit clients, and creating the Public Company Accounting Oversight Board (PCAOB)

Unqualified Audit Report: A type of report issued by a CPA firm at the completion of an audit. This report is issued when the CPA has gathered sufficient evidence and concludes that the financial statements being audited are in accordance with Generally Accepted Accounting Principles.

10-K Form: A form used to submit annual financial statement information to the SEC.

10-Q Form: A form used to submit quarterly financial statement information to the SEC.

Chapter 12

Fraud, Abuse and Embezzlement

Fraud is a knowing misrepresentation of material fact (or concealment of a material fact) done to induce another to act to his or her detriment. In the medical context, fraud is often committed in billing. When a physician bills for a procedure which the physician did not perform, or "upcodes" or charges for more than the physician performed, the physician has committed fraud to the insurance company. The insurance company received a misrepresentation of a material fact (a procedure not performed, or a procedure "upcoded"), the insurance company reasonably relied on the billing received, and the insurance company was damaged when it paid the physician more than the insurance company would have if the billing had been correct.

Fraud and abuse are often spoken of together. Practically, whether an action is fraud (a civil tort or a criminal act) or abuse (not a basis for a civil lawsuit or a criminal charge) largely depends on the intent of the party, the repetitiveness of the act, and the amount of money involved. Mere negligence in billing is not intentional and usually constitutes abuse rather than fraud. Repeated episodes of negligent billing have been held to constitute reckless conduct, which is tantamount to intentional behavior (fraud).

Embezzlement is the fraudulent taking or theft of property owned by another. In the medical context, embezzlement occurs when an employee steals money belonging to the medical practice. If several professionals are incorporated and one of the professionals uses corporate money for personal, non-corporate expenses, the embezzlement is call defalcation. State laws mandate penalties for defalcation. According to the Association of Certified Fraud

Examiners, fraud and embezzlement occurs with 100 times greater frequency in small corporations (such as those typical of medical professional corporations) compared to large corporations.

Who comments embezzlement within a medical practice? The most common persons are usually managers and bookkeepers. Insurance billing staff members are usually next, followed by nurses and medical assistants. Even cleaning crew members have been found to have obtained and embezzled the money of the medical professional entities.

Embezzlement is much less likely to occur in offices with tight internal controls. Adhering to some basic rules will reduce, but not eliminate, the chance of falling victim to embezzlement.

Incoming mail should never be opened by the person making deposits or maintaining accounts receivable records. It is relatively easy to cover theft when the perpetrator only both receives the incoming payments and controls the accounts receivable.

Checks received in the incoming mail should be copied immediately by the person opening the mail. Doing this creates a record of revenue received in the mail. Copies of these checks should be safely secured beyond the reach of other employees, but should be available for audit purposes.

Bank statements should only be opened by the health care provider managing the practice. If this is not possible, mailing the bank statements to the accountant's office should be considered. The individual receiving the bank statements should neither open the mail (and copy the checks received), nor have authority to control accounts receivable.

Arriving supplies should be checked against the packing slip by someone other than the person who ordered the supplies. The managing health care provider should always approve orders for supplies, other than those routinely ordered. Of those routinely ordered, the managing health care provider should occasionally "spot check" the routine supplies order to confirm the quantities and prices are correct.

The managing health care provider should never write the expense checks, but should examine the checks along with the accompanying invoice before signing the checks. Delegating an individual in the practice the authority to sign checks creates a potential position to abuse that authority. This can be mitigated by segregating that person from the other financial functions in the office. The delegated check signer should not be involved in opening the mail, billing, collections, or bank deposits. Some busy health care providers utilize an independent bookkeeper to write checks and "spot audit" the business details of the medical practice.

The above suggestions involve segregation of duties involving the income and expenses of the practice. Segregation of duties is a fundamental business practice and part of every prudent medical practice. Internal accounting controls must also be maintained within the medical practice.

The person opening the mail should stamp the checks received "For Deposit Only" before copying the checks. Both sides of checks should be copied. Once checked have been stamped for deposit only, banks should not cash the check for cash money. If the embezzler deposits the check into his or a co-conspirator's bank account, there is a paper trail.

Require all patients receive a numbered receipt for payments and that a copy of those receipts be maintained in numerical order at the practice. The receipts should be audited occasionally to confirm that all front office financial transactions receipts are present.

Keep petty cash and the change drawers separate so there cannot be any co-mingling. Co-mingling makes accurate auditing impossible and encourages petty theft. Over time, petty theft becomes grand theft.

Review deposits on the bank statement and reconcile to the manual or computer totals. Daily revenue totals should match deposits on bank statements.

Compare current period revenues and expenses to prior periods. Unexplained reductions in revenue or increase in expenses must be investigated. Computer bookkeeping programs are excellent for this.

Specific subaccounts can be graphed and tracked easily. Aberrations should become apparent early.

Have your accountant, who must be experienced in accounting for medical practices, review the practice's financial statement at least quarterly. No matter how financially facile the medical practitioner, a periodic review of the financial status of the practice by a professional (your accountant) will confirm the business aspect of the medical practice is sound.

Keep all blank checks and deposit slips in a secure location. Always use numerically sequenced checks. A blank check can be used by the cleaver embezzler to steal small amounts of money on a continuing basis, or a relatively large amount from the practice for the bolder embezzler. If checks are not always written in sequence, it may be more difficult to detect the theft.

All employees, including those involved in the business side of the medical practice, should be cross trained. One never knows when a particular employee will be victim to some unforeseen adverse event. The practice must be able to continue to function relatively smoothly with any one individual absent. Cross training insures a degree of internal integrity not present if a "critically important" employee, such as the chief billing clerk or the office manager, is the only one able to perform a vital business function.

The managing health care provider should assume certain responsibilities:

- Signing all checks and confirming the accompanying receipts are reasonable and accurate. The managing health care provider must assure that the invoice is legitimate. A common practice of embezzlers is to have checks written to a dummy business for products or services that appear necessary to conduct the medical practice. The embezzler, or a conspirator, controls the bank account of the dummy business, which is drained routinely. One other health care provider may have check writing authority (if there is more than one health care provider in the business) in case of vacation or illness. A health care provider who gives a spouse check writing authority in the business invites another layer to marital stress. This arrangement works well, until it doesn't!

- Review all business credit card statements, line by line, for accuracy and validity. Review cancelled checks periodically to determine that they match the invoice and to assure the amounts have not been altered.
- Avoid the use of signature stamps. The danger of misuse far outweighs the small time saved signing your name.
- Occasionally audit invoices against packing slips and check amounts in a manner that all employees are aware you are doing so.
- All bad debts to be forgone, or receivables to be sent to collections, should be individually authorized by the managing medical provider.
- Perform background checks on potential employees before offering them a position. It may be prudent to engage the services of a company which specializes in background checks.

What are some of the warning signs that an employee may be stealing?

- Patients complain about the practice's billings. Patients may receive more than one billing for the same service rendered.
- A refusal of an employee to take a vacation. Employees should take time off and their cross trained alternate should perform the duties of the vacationer. A policy and procedure manual can be very helpful in assuring routine procedures are performed as directed in the manual. Deviations from standard procedure should be permitted only with the signed or initialed written concurrence of the managing medical provider.
- Be very suspicious about employees who are territorial about their work. An office manager or billing clerk

who always locks their door whenever they are not in their office may herald malfeasance. An employee who locks his or her office when going on vacation and tells the other employees not to enter or touch anything in that office because he or she is the only one who knows where everything is, should arouse suspicion in the medical care provider's mind. Cross training employees should avoid this situation. If one employee becomes overloaded with work, the cross trained employee should be available to assist. If one employee becomes ill, the practice cannot cease to perform essential functions – the cross trained employee should be able to assume those functions.

- Staff taking work home may appear to be dedicated diligence in an employee. The prudent medical office provider should be very suspicious of this activity and not permit it. Taking work home provides the embezzler time and space to manipulate office finances. Such opportunity may not be available in the office.

- Beware of employees demonstrating "new" riches, such as a car the employee should not be affordable on the employee's salary, the new house or condo, the recently acquired recreational vehicle, or the new fancy designer clothes. Most embezzlers do not put their ill-gotten gains in hidden, secret bank accounts in foreign tax havens. Embezzlers generally are compelled to spend at least some of their newly acquired wealth.

- Books and financial papers that are in a confused or messy state, especially when the financial books and bank statements rarely match, indicate sloppy internal accounting practices at a minimum, and possibly signal embezzlement. Bank statements and internal finances should always reconcile. When they do not, your accountant should be consulted to help with the reconciliation. An inability to provide your accountant with correct or complete information in a timely manner also signals a lack of competence in the business accounting, at a minimum.

- Vendors who complain about payments being incorrect or chronically late should stimulate an investigation. While a common ploy of embezzlers is to work with a dishonest vendor (paying more for the products than they actually cost, splitting the overpayment), honest vendors will refuse to cooperate with a fraudulent or embezzlement scheme. Be certain to talk with a vendor who specifically asks to speak with the managing health care provider. Look specifically for a sudden increase in a vendor's price. There is much to commend the standard commercial practice of obtaining three independent quotes for any new product or service. Be cautious about vendors who are "friends" of an office worker.
- Medical care providers should be suspicious when, for no objective reason, income begins to decrease. If the amount of work is relatively the same, income should be relatively constant, and expenses should be roughly the same. Thus, net income should be relatively stable.

What should the managing health care provider do if employee theft is suspected? A surprising number of physicians have reported they suspected theft, but just didn't want to confront the long-time, "loyal" employee, or they just didn't know how to approach the situation. This reticence almost always leads to substantially greater losses than would otherwise have occurred.

If you suspected theft, call your accountant, or a fraud/embezzlement specialist, to conduct an audit of the medical practice's finances. Hostility in the cooperation of key business employees in the audit is common when cash or assets are missing. Don't be deterred by employees who attempt to raise guilt in the medical provider with questions such as, "don't you trust me"? These issues are not questions of trust; they are issues of prudent business practices.

Because anyone in the medical practice may be involved in embezzlement, the prudent health care provider should "position bond" any position in the office having contact with the business side of the practice. In some small practices, that may mean every employee. The costs of such bonding are usually not prohibitive. Your insurance agent can obtain quotes for you. By bonding an employee, you can assure recovery of at least a portion of the money stolen. The bonding company, not having a personal relationship with the employee, will not be reluctant to push for prosecution of the thieving employee. Health care providers are notorious about forgiving an employee for embezzlement. It is not uncommon for the managing health care provider to continue employment of the embezzler, after the embezzler repeated promises "not to do it again." Or the managing health care provider decides to continue the thief's employment, so that the employee "can pay back the money stolen." These strategies rarely are successful, and the dishonest employee often continues to steal.

In these situations, it may be prudent to seek the services of an attorney specializing in health law or a labor attorney. The managing health care provider should discharge the employee in manner consistent with Federal and State laws. The discharged employee will often threaten repercussions. The attorney will seek to minimize these.

Some health care providers find themselves in situations where the embezzler has "something over them." Perhaps they have had, or are having, an illicit sexual relationship with the employee. Perhaps the employee is aware of some illegal billing practices by the health care provider. Embezzling employees will often leverage these situations to retain their employment status and intimidate the health care provider from taking any action. These situations almost always lead to disaster for the health care provider. The embezzling employee often feels secure in their "right" to steal from the practice. A health care provider in this situation should surreptitiously contact a competent attorney. Remember that conversations between an attorney and his or her client are confidential and protected under law. The health care provider and the attorney will develop a best strategy to confront the situation.

The worst action by a health care provider in one of these situations is no action. The health care provider becomes the financial slave of the embezzling employee. Whatever the embezzling employee "has over you," a good attorney can ameliorate the damages, and, most importantly, help extract you from an untenable situation.

Embezzlement is very common in health care practices. Do not be shocked by your most trusted, long term employee being the source of the embezzlement. Learn from your mistakes. Discourage embezzlement by operating your health care business with prudent precautions, safeguards, and with tight accounting controls.

Appendix

Using QuickBooks® in the Medical Field

Julie A. Mucha-Aydlott, CFE and Author of

"I have QuickBooks, Now What?"

There are many accounting software packages available for use in small businesses. **QuickBooks®** has probably been the most used software for small businesses to date. Although there is not a QuickBooks® version for the medical field, there are many versions of medical billing software available that can be merged or imported into QuickBooks® allowing better tracking of the accounts receivable and billing function. One can check with his or her medical billing software to see if there is an option for importing the company's data into QuickBooks®.

This brief chapter on QuickBooks® is not intended to teach step by step instructions on how to use the software. Rather, this chapter demonstrates how QuickBooks® may permit one to get the most benefit from the development and use of financial reports. There are many good books on QuickBooks® that can help one better understand the details of the software.

Setting up QuickBooks® correctly in the beginning is the most important step._—It is best to hire a professional familiar with QuickBooks® to install and set up the software. Mistakes made at this stage can result in large expenditures of money to correct the consequences of those errors. In establishing QuickBooks® in a medical practice, the following is necessary:

- Know what business type you are – are you a LLC, Sole Proprietor, S-Corp or C-Corp?

- Know what accounting method your tax returns are filed on or if you are new ask your CPA what accounting method you will be using. If you carry receivables, you are set up as an accrual method

- Have your records readily available

  - ✓ Taxpayer ID number

  - ✓ Business loan statements

  - ✓ Credit card statements

  - ✓ Bank statements

  - ✓ Billing reports and receivables due

  - ✓ Vendor bills due

  - ✓ Payroll reports – if an outside service is used

  - ✓ Fixed assets – Cars, Medical Equipment, Office Equipment, etc.

In order to create a clean set of books, or to go back and fix the mistakes made in the first place, one needs to be comfortable with the software or hire a professional who is comfortable with the software. Except for the most facile of medical computer geeks, hiring a professional to install and implement QuickBooks® is most practical.

Your QuickBooks® company file has several reports, all of which are easily generated. The most important reports are discussed below. One advantage of QuickBooks® is that the medical professional can generate these reports whenever he or she wishes.

Balance Sheet - Your balance sheet is a very important report for your business. Not only should it keep one up-dated on how much cash and other assets that the business has, but it will also show the current and long term liabilities, as well as equity. Banks use a balance sheet to determine the financial strength of a business. If the numbers don't make sense or the ratios are off because of messy bookkeeping, lenders won't be confident in the financial stability of the company. The following balance sheet is just an assumption, but will show what some general balance sheet items are and where they are listed. This balance sheet shows accounts receivable which can be omitted in modified cash basis accounting, or can be pulled from your billing software. Remember, in modified cash basis accounting, income is recognized when it is received, and liabilities are recognized when they are incurred.

Medical Practices, PC

BALANCE SHEET

As of September 30, 2011

Assets		30 Sep 2011
Current Assets		
Checking/Savings		
Business Checking		21,672.15
Business Savings		17,838.40
Total Checking /Savings		39,150.55
Accounts Receivable		
Accounts Receivable		75,037.26
Total Accounts Receivable		75,037.26
Other Current Assets		
Employee Advances		2,001.25
Prepaid Expenses		
Federal Tax	5,000.00	
Equipment Lease	1,018.71	
Total Prepaid Expenses		6,018.71
Organizational Costs		370.00
Deposits		2,600.00
Total Other Current Assets		10,989.96
Total Current Assets		125,537.77
Fixed Assets		
Fixed Assets		
Vehicles	76,648.98	
Medical Equipment	37,698.38	
Office Equipment	7,131.60	
Office Furniture & Fixtures	1,939.64	
Accumulated Depreciation	-89,363.00	
Total Fixed Assets		34,055.60
Total Fixed Assets		34,055.60
Total Fixed Assets		159,593.37

Medical Practices, PC
BALANCE SHEET
As of September 30, 2011

Liabilities		30 Sep 2011
Current Liabilities		
Accounts Payable		
Accounts Payable		19,547.87
Total Accounts Payable		19,547.87
Credit Cards		
Credit Card		11,789.82
Total Credit Cards		11,789.82
Other Current Liabilities		
Payroll Liabilities		249.62
Total Other Current Liabilities		249.62
Total Current Liabilities		31,587.31
Long Term Liabilities		
Business Line of Credit		40,563.55
Auto Loan		5,837.75
Equipment Notes		
Equipment Lease 001	35,348.68	
Equipment Lease 003	8,401.20	
Total Equipment Notes		43,749.88
Total Long Term Liabilities		90,151.18
Total Liabilities		121,738.49
Equity		
Retained Earnings		-27,301.72
Partner Contributions		
Dr. Smith	27,262.50	
Dr. Jones	26,262.50	
Total Partner Contributions		53,525.00
Partner Distributions		
Dr. Jones	-2,000	
Total Partner Distributions		-2,000.00
Net Income		13,631.60
Total Equity		37,854.88
Total Liabilities & Equity		159,593.37

Income Statement - Your profit and loss will show how much the company has collected for medical services, how much has been spent on operations and how much is owed by the company, presenting a net profit or loss per period. In QuickBooks® it is easy to tailor your reports to fit the business. In the sample profit and loss report, the medical supplies average almost 11% of the total income. This particular report is perfect for watching your company's trends from one year to the next. You will be able to track changes in your income vs. changes in your expenses which makes it so much easier to analyze any significant deviations.

12:43 AM
01/09/11
Accrual Basis

Medical Practices, PC
Profit & Loss
October 2010 through September 2011

	Oct '10 – Sep '11	% of Income
Ordinary Income / Expense		
Income		
Gross Income		
Standard Office Visit	341,665.59	62.1%
Preventive Visit	198,075.76	36%
Consultation	6,800.00	1.2%
Discounts	-70.00	-0%
Misc. Income	3,983.50	0.7%
Total Gross Income	550,454.85	100.0%
Total Income	550,454.85	100.0%
Gross Profit	550,454.85	100.0%
Expense		
Direct Costs		
Disposable Equipment	1,259.05	0.2%
Drugs & Medications	22,825.31	4.1%
General Supplies	4,924.87	0.9%
Lab Fees	11,016.06	2%
Linen Supplies	9,989.77	1.8%
Medical Forms	8,672.25	1.6%
Medical Supplies	59,459.55	10.8%
MR Supplies	9,187.30	1.7%
Other supplies: Portable X-rays	2,926.31	0.5%
Purchased Services Physician	908.50	0.2%
X-Ray Film	1,174.83	0.2%
Total Direct Costs	132,343.80	24%

Detailed General Ledger – The detailed general ledger is going to be the blueprint for all entries into the QuickBooks® data file. This is the report used to go back through each chart of account and make sure the entries are correct. It is a combination of the balance sheet and profit and loss report expanded showing everything in a single entry item. The following report is a snap shot of a detailed general ledger report. It keeps the year to date running totals as well as includes all of the information entered into your bookkeeping system.

2:48 PM
01/09/11
Accrual Basis

Medical Practices, PC

General Ledger

As of September 30, 2011

◦ Date ◦	Num ◦	Name ◦	Memo ◦	Debit ◦	Credit ◦	Balance ◦
Total Consulting						3,800.00
Total Professional Fees				616.40	0.00	6,091.80
Rent						39,000.00
09/05/2008	Aug 2008...	Commercial Rent	August 2008 late charge	250.00		39,250.00
09/10/2008	9/1-9/15/08	Commercial Rent	9/1/08-9/15/08	1,800.00		41,050.00
09/10/2008	9/16/08-10...	Commercial Rent	9/16/08-10/15/08	3,600.00		44,650.00
Total Rent				5,650.00	0.00	44,650.00
Repairs						72.00
Equipment Repairs						72.00
Total Equipment Repairs						72.00
Total Repairs						72.00
Telephone						7,493.97
09/09/2008	619-460-8...	Phone Service	Monthly service 8/23/08-9...	190.71		7,684.68
09/09/2008	Inv. 06867...	Cellular Service Inc	Inv. 0686740628	241.91		7,926.59
09/19/2008		Cable Communica...	Cox for high speed for com...	59.92		7,986.51
Total Telephone				492.54	0.00	7,986.51
Travel & Ent						1,584.42
Meals						1,584.42
09/10/2008	19497	Petty Cash	meals	36.76		1,621.18
09/26/2008	19510	Cash	Travel expense for trip to ...	200.00		1,821.18
Total Meals				236.76	0.00	1,821.18

Unpaid bills detail (Accounts Payable Report) - This shows the vendor invoice numbers, amount due, due date and running balance. An aged payable report shows the combined total due for that specific vendor and ages it by 30 to 90 days plus. Both reports are good, however seeing the detail can also allow for more specific budgeting and will allow one to see the actual due date.

Medical Practices, PC

Unpaid Bills Detail

As of September 30, 2011

Type	Date	Num	Due Date	Aging	Open Balance
Bill	09/26/2008	19 E1 181010	10/10/2008		74.25
Total Disposal Service					74.25
Electric Company					
Bill	09/26/2008		10/11/2008		222.13
Total Electric Company					222.13
Golden Insurance					
Bill	09/26/2008	Acct 600592330	10/12/2008		833.41
Total Golden Insurance					833.41
Integra Adhesives					
Bill	09/25/2008	Inv.38016	10/12/2008		90.00
Total Integra Adhesives					90.00
IPD Supplies					
Bill	09/25/2008	8290938-00	11/02/2008		4,415.92
Bill	09/25/2008	Inv. 8291255-00	11/13/2008		9,477.23
Total IPD Supplies					13,893.15
P&C Lab Supplies					
Bill	09/25/2008	McWephy	10/16/2008		492.34
Bill	09/02/2008		10/16/2008		662.41
Bill	09/15/2008		10/30/2008		226.28
Bill	09/15/2008		10/30/2008		1,600.69
Total P&C Lab Supplies					2,981.72

These reports not only are important to be on top of the company's finances, but to also see any deviations from one period to the next. If there is a financial problem, understanding business reports will help determine cash flow problems, overextending vendor credit as well as overall costs. QuickBooks® allows one to print files in a pdf format. One can print lengthy general ledgers and all reports to a pdf file and save it to a hard drive, as well as an external drive for a duplicate copy.

Year End Accounting and QuickBooks®

Taking time to reconcile your accounts, review your general ledger for mistakes and fix them, will put the medical professional in control of day to day bookkeeping, –and it will make year_end accounting that much easier. With QuickBooks® one can create an accountant's copy to send over to the company's CPA so that they can review all of your entries throughout the year. They will be able to post adjusting entries, record your depreciation and hand you back a flash drive with all of the changes that will balance to the company's tax return.

Also make sure you take the time to back up your company's financial data on a consistent basis. Re-entering in an entire year isn't fun when your computer happens to lose everything.

Accounting software, such as QuickBooks®, can be a time saver and money saver. It is much less expensive than an in-house bookkeeper. And, it permits the medical professional the opportunity to understand the business aspects of the company with minimal technical knowledge and competence in the science of accounting.

Index

Price/Earnings Ratio, 143
Professional corporations, 94
Proprietorships, sole proprietorships, 22
Public Company Accounting Oversight Board, 167

Q

Qualified Audit Report, 168
Quantifiable Information, 38
Quick Ratio, 131

R

Rate of Return on Investment, 143
Rate of Revenue Growth, 143
Realizable Value Principle, 39
Recognition Principle, 39
Recognize, 79
Relevant information, 39
Reliable Information, 40
Retained Earnings, 63
Revenue, 79
Review, 168

S

Sarbanes-Oxley Act (2002), 168
SEC, 39
Securities and Exchange Commission, 39
Separate Entities, 40
Short-term assets, 63
Sole Proprietorship, 94
Stable-Monetary-Unit Concept, 40
Statement of Retained Earnings, 22

T

Trial Balance, 122

U

Understandable Information, 40
Unqualified Audit Report, 168

V

Verifiable Information, 40

W

Working Capital, 131